# CONTENTS

## Tables

## Diagrams

# ACKNOWLEDGEMENTS

The authors would like to thank the young people, foster carers and social services staff who generously gave up their time, and without whose help this report would not have been possible. This project is indebted to the openness and honesty of all those who took part. The Children's Society would also like to thank the steering groups in each authority for their help and support in planning this project, and the young people, carers and staff who contributed to its development.

Thanks are also due to the researchers: Assia King, Janet Falk and James Brown for their expertise in interviewing young people and their carers, and to Joanna Ford who diligently transcribed all interviews and formatted them for data analysis.

## Terminology

Throughout this report the following terminology had been used:

- Young people     Refers to all children and young people regardless of age.

- Link worker     Refers to the placement worker supporting the foster carer. Terminology for this post varies across local authorities. Link workers may also be known as fostering support workers, fostering officers or family placement workers.

- Complaints procedure     This abbreviated term is used instead of Section 26 of The Children Act 1989 – The Representations and Complaints Procedure.

# FOREWORD

The majority of children in care now lives with foster carers. Fostering services depend upon the willingness of families and individuals in the community to share their homes and their lives with children and young people whose parents are temporarily or permanently unable to care for them. Foster carers also share their lives with a range of professionals with whom they work in partnership.

However, while the care of vulnerable children and young people is at the heart of fostering, the role of the foster carer goes beyond that. In our modern society, families come under pressure from a range of problems including poverty, ill health, drug and alcohol abuse, and relationship breakdowns.

By temporarily caring for children, and protecting them from such problems, foster carers give the families of these youngsters an opportunity to resolve their difficulties and be reunited with their children. Foster carers plan a vital role in keeping families together and it is obviously a source of great price when they see the children making progress towards successful adult lives, whether or not they eventually rejoin their families.

This, of course, does not mean that fostering is without its problems and so the timing and focus of The Children's Society report *Solving Problems in Foster Care* is very welcome. We know that foster carers and young people need better support in placements to be able to solve problems as they arise – and, as this report identifies, access to effective complaints procedures and advocacy services are an essential part of this. Local authorities and independent providers of fostering services have a responsibility to offer appropriate training and support to their foster carers in the context of a properly managed service – and we in government need to make sure that providers have the necessary tools to be able to do so.

There are a number of important initiatives under way to bring about widespread improvements to the quality and delivery of children's services, such as Quality Protects, the new Fostering Services Regulations and National Minimum Standards, and the recently announced Choice Protects review of placement choice and fostering service. This is a major programme of work designed to deliver better outcomes for children who are cared for away from home.

Every single one of use has an interest in making sure that children thrive, and are helped to grow up into healthy and socially responsible adults. I would therefore like to extend my thanks to The Children's Society for this report, which is a significant contribution to the debate around the development of better children's services.

**Rt Hon. Jacqui Smith** MP
MINISTER OF STATE FOR HEALTH

# Summary

## 1. Aims

1. To establish how young people in foster care solve problems.

2. To establish how foster carers solve problems.

3. To establish how social services managers are informed and influenced by the views of young people in foster care and by those of their carers.

4. To explore the role of the Representations and Complaints Procedure within foster care and, in particular, why young people in foster care and their carers rarely use the complaints procedure.

## 2. Methodology

This study was carried out in co-operation with three local authorities in the north of England. Interviews took place with:

- 61 young people (aged 8 to 18 years)
- 56 foster carers
- 18 social workers
- 18 link workers
- 16 managers.

Participation was entirely voluntary. Young people, foster carers and social services staff took an active part in the planning and preparation of interview schedules used. Findings were shared with young people and foster carers, and their views incorporated into comments on policy and practice issues.

## 3. Summary of findings

### Overview of young people's concerns, support and reliance

- Most young people's concerns relate directly to issues about living with a substitute family, with 48 per cent of concerns expressed about the welfare of their birth families and the contact young people had with various family members. Concerns ranged from: a wish to be with, or see more of, their parents; parents' behaviour; the health of grandparents (particularly if they were known to have been ill); worry about siblings placed elsewhere; and general feelings about the lack of information about their extended families.

- Other worries included anxieties over their long-term future, school or college exams, and career prospects.

- Young people also expressed concern about maintaining their social life and friendships. Although these are common concerns for most young people, they are likely to be compounded for young people in care, who may experience several moves of placement.

- The majority of young people in foster care (about 85 per cent) feel well supported in their placements, looking primarily to their foster carers for support. A fluctuating minority group of about 15 per cent of young people do not feel well supported and tend to rely on the adults around them.

## Young people and problem solving

- Young people use a variety of strategies to sort out problems and involve their foster carers, especially in resolving domestic issues. They rely on social workers when there are concerns about contact with their birth family, but keeping in touch with friends is something that many young people take responsibility for themselves. However, if young people's familiar support networks are disrupted (for example, preoccupation of their carer with another child; absence or change of social worker or change of placement), young people express low levels of confidence that their problems will be resolved.

- Foster carers demonstrate considerable responsibility in helping young people resolve concerns and are perhaps more involved than young people acknowledge.

- Social workers' involvement in problem solving depends on the type of problem concerned and on their relationship with the young person.

- Foster carers and social workers recognise the division of young people into well supported and less well-supported groups. Foster carers are not always happy with the support offered by social workers. Social workers recognise the scarcity of foster placements and that, sometimes, young people are left in unsatisfactory situations, feeling unsupported.

- The most important factor in supportive relationships for young people is good dialogue. Young people generally look to their foster carers and, to a lesser extent, their social workers for this support, and expect carers and social workers to work closely together. We have termed this network of young person, foster carer and social worker the 'core triangle of support'.

- Problem solving for young people takes place almost entirely within this core triangle of support.

- For the minority unsupported group, there is little access to any alternative forms of support outside the core triangle identified, yet members of this group are unlikely to confide in either their carers or their social workers.

- Factors that hinder support for young people include being ignored and having concerns minimised by adults (especially foster carers and social workers).

- Young people describe taking considerable responsibility themselves where they lack support from adults, blaming, for example, their own behaviour or bottling up concerns.

- Foster carers identify two major themes that contribute to successful problem solving: resourcefulness and persistence of carers; and good social work intervention.

- Where supportive links are weak, foster carers identify poor social work intervention as the main cause, but also acknowledge their own limitations. Where necessary, foster carers will enlist help from outside the core triangle of support (i.e. from link workers and managers).

- Social workers recognise good parenting by the foster carers and good relationships between social workers and carers as key to good problem solving. Where support is lacking for young people, social workers identify the main hindrances as poor parenting skills of foster carers and their own inability to engage effectively with young people.

- Link workers mention little direct contact with young people, as their role is to support the foster carer. Middle and senior managers only become involved in problem solving if matters are brought to their attention by carers or by their own officers. Young people rarely, if ever, contact them directly.

## Foster carers and problem solving

- The majority of carers feel well supported and accept considerable responsibility for resolving problems.

- Although foster carers look to their link worker for ongoing support, it is the involvement of social workers that has a much more significant impact on the outcome of problem solving – a view shared by link workers. Where social workers' relationships with young people are good, they are likely to be good with the carer and vice versa.

- Link workers vary their involvement in problem solving for foster carers, depending on the problem and how skilled carers are in problem resolution, but they take a significant role in liaison with social workers.

- Link workers identify communication and team working as the most effective strategy in problem solving.

- As with young people, social services staff recognise the involvement of successive management layers in problem solving for foster carers.

## Young people's participation and influence

- Just over half the young people and foster carers interviewed believe that young people's views are fed back to social services managers, but the vast majority of staff, and a sizeable minority of young people and carers, do not believe senior managers are well informed about young people's views.

- Although young people's views may be fed back through reviews, via social workers and via foster carers, there is no evidence that this information is collated and fed into management processes, thus leaving planners and policy makers with no overview of the voices from foster care.

- Young people, foster carers and social services staff see young people's views as having little influence on the fostering service. Most managers believe young people's influence is minimal or non-existent.
- Young people, foster carers and social workers felt that the most constructive way of improving young people's influence is for social workers to spend more time with young people and their families.

## Foster carers' participation and influence

- A small majority of foster carers and managers believe foster carers' views are fed back into the system. But the vast majority of link workers and social workers, plus a sizeable minority of carers, do not believe social services managers are well informed about foster carers' views.
- Foster carers believe their level of influence is only slightly more effective than that of young people, yet 70 per cent of managers feel foster carers are influential.
- The improvement foster carers most frequently called for was to have their views listened to and respected more by social workers.

## Young people and the complaints procedure

- Over half the young people have no knowledge of the complaints procedure. Although there is agreement that there is less to complain about in foster care, real fear exists about the consequences of complaining.
- Social services staff see the complaints procedure as adversarial and unhelpful in problem solving.
- There is poor collation of informal complaints and those raised at reviews, leaving managers with little information about the level and type of complaints raised by young people in foster care.

## Foster carers and the complaints procedure

- The majority of carers are aware of the procedure although there is wide variation in levels of knowledge and understanding.
- Over 80 per cent of carers have no experience of making a complaint or encouraging a young person to do so.
- Foster carers and link workers highlight the success of day-to-day problem solving as the main reason why the complaints procedure is rarely used. There is an acknowledgement that the fear of possible consequences also contributes significantly to foster carers' reluctance to make formal complaints.
- There is a culture of institutional disapproval, which prevents the complaints procedure being regarded as an acceptable mode of problem solving within foster care.

# 4. Recommendations

- Social services should be proactive in expanding the support network for young people in foster care. This may include dependable family members, young people's friends, peer support schemes, supportive teachers and independent services (such as children's rights services, advocacy services and independent visitors). Social services need to identify who a young person's natural allies are and support these relationships. Social services managers need to open up direct lines of communication with young people in foster care.

- Social services need to pay greater attention to the continuity of social workers for young people. This should be taken into account in terms of recruitment and retention policies, and plans for reorganisation of services.

- Social services need to openly acknowledge and value the central role that foster carers play in problem solving. All carers from the outset should be equipped – through training and support – with the skills needed.

- Foster carers should be trained and empowered to act as advocates for young people. There needs to be clarification of roles and expectations – achieved perhaps through a contact system that recognises carers as partners in the provision of services.

- Social services need to promote the importance of direct work skills with young people – ensuring social workers and foster carers continue to develop their skills in listening and responding to young people's needs and concerns.

- Social workers need to acknowledge the key role they play within fostering – in terms of problem solving, maintaining family contact and identifying natural allies – and this role needs to be emphasised in professional training.

- With young people in foster care accounting for only a small minority of social workers' caseloads, social services must ensure social workers develop their expertise in this field.

- Young people should be informed of the roles and responsibilities of foster carers and social services, so that they are clear who to approach in different circumstances if they have a problem.

- Social workers need to take greater responsibility in passing on the views of young people to managers.

- Review systems need to be much more child-focused to encourage and enable young people to take part and voice their views.

- Local authorities need to ensure appropriate links are made between fostering units and social work teams and that there are forums through which information is freely exchanged, and passed on to senior managers and policy makers.

- Social services must establish systematic methods for collecting and collating the views of young people in foster care. These need to be fed into management processes to ensure fostering services are responsive to young people's expressed views.

- Information about the complaints procedure needs to be specifically targeted at young people in foster care and their foster carers to ensure they have knowledge and access to the complaints procedure.

- The culture of institutional disapproval regarding the use of the complaints procedure needs to be challenged at all levels in the local authority. Most importantly, disapproval at social worker, link worker and line management level needs to be actively challenged as a priority.

- Local authority councillors need to take on board their responsibilities as corporate parents with regard to listening and responding to the needs of young people in foster care.

# 1

# INTRODUCTION

*Research into foster care shows that the service on the whole works well,
but this is probably despite what we do, not because of it.* (Berridge, 1997)

## Background

In 1999 Ena Fry of the National Foster Care Association wrote that 'as we approach
the end of the century, foster care is in crisis' (Fry, 1999, p.204). Indeed we can speak
with some confidence of a crisis in the entire care system. One symptom of this crisis
was a series of high-profile 'scandals', mainly but not exclusively in children's homes,
throughout the 1970s, 1980s and 1990s which triggered the publication of a number
of key state-sponsored reports. The three main reports into these scandals are:

- Sir William Utting's *Children in the Public Care* (HMSO,1991)
- Utting's follow-up report *People Like Us* (HMSO, 1997)
- the report of the Waterhouse Inquiry, *Lost in Care* (The Stationery Office, 2000).

The findings of these reports and many others (*see* Frost, Mills and Stein, 1999) add
up to a sad indictment of a system that seems to have consistently failed children and
young people in the public care.

How can we move on from this period of scandal and crisis in a clear and
coherent manner? First of all we need to recognise that the system has failed and
abused many children and young people, and then we need to develop a system
which ensures that children and young people are centre stage – that the care system
listens to, responds to, and empowers those it is designed, in the words of The
Children Act 1989, to 'look after' (*see* Fry, 1999).

Following the publication of *People Like Us* the Government launched a major
policy initiative known as Quality Protects. The title of this initiative reflects one of
Utting's major conclusions, which is that 'the best safeguard is an environment of
overall excellence' (1997, p.1). Quality Protects is a complex programme that
involves wholesale organisational and cultural change. The objectives of the initiative,
as initially outlined in *Modernising Social Services* (Department of Health, 1998) and
later revised, are listed below:

## Quality Protects objectives

1. To ensure that children are securely attached to carers capable of providing safe and effective care for the duration of childhood.

2. To ensure that children are protected from emotional, physical and sexual abuse and neglect (significant harm).

3. To ensure that children in need gain maximum life chance benefits from educational opportunities, health care and social care.

4. To ensure that children looked after gain maximum life chance benefits from educational opportunities, health care and social care.

5. To ensure that young people leaving care, as they enter adulthood, are not isolated and participate socially and economically as citizens.

6. To ensure that children with specific social needs arising out of disability or a health condition are living in families or other appropriate settings in the community where their assessed needs are adequately met and reviewed.

7. To ensure that referral and assessment processes discriminate effectively between different types and levels of need and produce a timely service response.

8. To actively involve users and carers in planning services and in tailoring individual packages of care; and to ensure effective mechanisms are in place to handle complaints.

9. To ensure through regulatory powers and duties that children in regulated services are protected from harm and poor care standards.

10. To ensure that social care workers are appropriately skilled, trained and qualified and to promote the uptake of training at all levels.

11. To maximise the benefit to service users from the resources available, and to demonstrate the effectiveness and value for money of the care and support provided, and allow for choice and different responses for different needs and circumstances.

The implementation of Quality Protects, which involves training, monitoring and service development, has been funded at a cost of £885 million, over a five-year period. Quality Protects forms the key reference point for the future of the looked after children system. Central to the Quality Protects Initiative is the active involvement of young people.

In this study we aim to assess how young people in foster care are involved, given that, today, foster care is the predominant form of care for looked after children and young people. While the number of fostered children has remained remarkably stable throughout the 1980s and 1990s – with between 32,000 and 35,000 children being fostered at any given time – as the number of residential places has decreased the proportionate role of foster care has significantly increased. In 1980 about one-third of looked after children were fostered, increasing to one-half in 1985 and to about two-thirds in 1998 (Department of Health, 1999).

We want to know how young people in foster care are listened to and involved – ranging from day-to-day decisions to wider decisions involving policy making. As Sir William Utting pointed out, 'despite the predominance of foster care for looked after children, there is relatively little data on it. It has a lower profile than residential care and less media and policy attention' (1997, p.31). It is important therefore that we continue to develop and extend what we know about foster care.

## About this study

This study grew out of the activities of a Children's Society project – the Children's Resources Project in York – which has the following aims and objectives:

1. To take a leading role in promoting the rights of all children and young people who come into contact with public care and legal systems.

2. To enable children and young people to influence decisions, systems and practices that affect their lives.

3. To demonstrate that child-centred approaches, together with systematic planning, lead to better outcomes for children and young people.

In 1996 the project commissioned a piece of research on the operation of the complaints system for looked after children. This was published in 1998 as *Cause for Complaint – the Complaints Procedure for Young People in Care* (Wallis and Frost, 1998). One conclusion of that report was that, 'although foster care is by far the most predominant form of care for separated children and young people, residents in this setting are underrepresented in those making complaints' (1998, p.65). This study aims to broaden our understanding of what is happening here. Why should it be that young people in foster care are less likely to use the complaints system? What is happening in terms of the wider issues of negotiation and problem solving? What follows is the outcome of this research.

## Aims and objectives

*1. To establish how young people in foster care solve problems*

- We look at young people's general perceptions about their placement and the support they receive.

- We identify the kinds of issues that currently concern them.

- We look at how young people in foster care sort out problems they face – including who young people choose to rely on and the strategies they use to sort out different problems.

- We explore whether foster carers, children's social workers and senior social services managers share young people's views and expectations.
- We identify interventions that are successful in problem solving and those that have proved unhelpful.

*2. To establish how foster carers solve problems*

- We look at how foster carers problem solve – who they rely on, and what strategies they use, and whether these vary from strategies they might use if young people raise concerns with them.
- We look at whether link workers and social services managers share the same views and expectations as foster carers.
- We identify the helpful and unhelpful interventions in problem solving for foster carers.

*3. To establish how social services managers are informed and influenced by the views of young people in foster care and their carers*

Quality Protects' key tasks require the local authority to have a mechanism for hearing the views of children and young people about the services they receive. The research will contribute to the understanding of the routes via which foster carers and young people in foster care currently feed back their views to social services managers and how influential their views are.

*4. To explore the role within foster care of the Representations and Complaints Procedure and, in particular, why young people in foster care and foster carers rarely use the complaints procedure*

The Representations and Complaints Procedure was introduced in The Children Act 1989 and implemented in 1991. As well as an avenue for redressing poor services, the complaints procedure was also intended to act as a safeguard for young people living away from home. The documentation of complaints from, or on behalf of, young people also provides social services departments with valuable management information about those aspects of its services that need improvement. This study seeks to evaluate how well the complaints procedure fills these roles within the fostering service.

- We look at the level of awareness young people and foster carers have about the complaints procedure and where that knowledge is gained.
- We identify the kind of issues they might use the complaints procedure to address.
- We look at why the procedure is so seldom used in foster care compared with residential care.

# Review of the literature

### Young people and problem solving

Young people in foster care not only have to deal with all the normal trials and tribulations of growing up, they also have to deal with separation from their families, emotional conflicts and uncertainty about their future. All this happens within a substitute family, with various professionals coming and going, and varying amounts of contact with their birth families. Establishing who young people rely on, and who they choose to talk to, will help us begin to understand how young people in foster care try to sort out the problems they face.

Compared with the literature on residential care there is very little published research on fostering and even less focusing on the views of the young people fostered. Rowe *et al.* (1984) found that most of the children they interviewed were extremely positive about their foster homes and stressed the importance of having a family, and Colton (1989) found that fostered young people perceived their foster carers to be their primary source of support. Among the best things about being in care identified by young people in a study by Shaw (1998) were having someone to talk to and someone to help with their problems. Morris and Wheatley (1994), however, identified family contact and siblings as important sources of support for 'looked after' young people. They also found a number of factors that influenced children's choice of who they approached with specific problems, notably the age of the child, the number of previous placements they had had and the types of problems they were experiencing. Generally, the younger the child, or the more settled they were, the more likely they were to talk to their carer about problems. Those over 14, though, were more likely than others to confide in a friend. Others, such as Bond (1999), Ibidun (2000) and MacLeod (1997), also suggest that young people may prefer to talk to their peers rather than an adult.

As well as foster carers, family and friends, young people in foster care should all have an allocated social worker. Their primary role is to safeguard and promote the young person's welfare and to monitor and actively progress the young person's care plan. Social workers are expected to undertake regular visits to young people in foster care and ensure that they have time to meet with the young person alone (National Foster Care Association, 1999). They therefore represent an important source of support for young people. Studies such as those by Fletcher (1993), McTeigue (1998) and Baldry and Kemmis (1998) reported that the majority of young people in foster care were positive about their social workers, valuing the relationship they had with them. Listening, getting things done and having a genuine interest in them were some of the qualities young people appreciated in a good social worker (Baldry and Kemmis, 1998).

However, in Fletcher's study, one in ten young people in foster care said there were no good things about their social worker (Fletcher, 1993, p.16). In The Dolphin Project (1993) young people reported feeling closer to their foster carers than to their social workers and many had great difficulty in getting in touch with their social workers. Triseliotis *et al.* (2000) reported some foster carers as being frustrated by the lack of availability of social workers and that they associated this with social workers' lack of concern for the children. Some foster carers suggested that because social workers were subject to quick turnover, they did not always know the child well enough to be able to share information or help in problem solving.

This is borne out in the study by MacLeod (1996) into calls received by Childline. From March 1995 to March 1996, the charity received 484 calls from young people in foster care. Young people said over and over again that they could not confide their concerns to their carers and social workers because they did not see their social workers; or felt that they were not taken seriously, that everyone would find out, or that the adults did not have time for them. Young people seemed unable to approach their social workers about relationship difficulties in their foster families, thinking that they risked losing yet another family if they asked for help or identified a problem. The highest proportion of calls was about being in care itself, and family relationships also featured highly in young people's concerns. Those calling from foster care were particularly troubled by relationships with their families (MacLeod, 1996). A major finding of McAuley's (1996) in-depth study of 19 young people in foster care was young people's preoccupation and identification with their birth families over time. Despite many difficulties in the home situation, McAuley points to evidence that young people worry about their parents' welfare. Studies by McTeigue (1998) and Johnson *et al.* (1994) also demonstrate that young people in foster care miss and worry about their birth families.

Clearly for the young people calling Childline the support needed to discuss their problems was missing. Childline estimates that it receives calls from about 1.1 per cent of young people in foster care, but the majority of these are from girls aged 10 to 18 years. The charity is concerned that boys and younger children may be deterred from asking for help when they need it most (MacLeod, 1996). Rowe *et al.* (1984) found some disturbing pockets of unhappiness, fears and worries among young people in foster care. Foster parents and social workers were often unaware of the young people's anxieties and painful feelings. Rowe concluded that, for the most part, fostered young people saw their social workers as potential rather than actual sources of information and support. Unless they were in direct contact with their own families, they relied primarily on their foster carers. Only a few young people saw their social workers as playing a significant part in their lives (Rowe *et al.*, 1984).

## Young people's participation and influence

For social services to ensure that the right support is available to children and young people in foster care, they need to hear from young people themselves about what their concerns and needs are. The Dolphin Project (1993) explored the process of involving young people in the development and provision of services and found that young people had highly relevant things to say about the services they needed. Article 12 of the UN Convention on the Rights of the Child 1989 sends out a very strong message about the importance of listening to the child's voice. The convention expects that the child should be free to express their views (Kelly and Gilligan, 2000).

Triseliotis *et al.* (2000) found, however, that 'none of the 32 Scottish local authorities had formal systems in place for the representation on committees or working groups of young people from foster care. Instead, great reliance was placed on social workers consulting with young people and conveying their views back to various working groups. Bond and Pickerden (2000) reported that other local authorities relied heavily on the review systems in terms of seeking young people's views. This, in turn, relies on the ability of children and young people to express opinions, which often rests again on the quality of the relationship between the child and the social worker. If the child and the social worker do not have a good relationship, there is often no alternative way for the child's voice to be heard (Bond and Pickerden, 2000).

The local authority, as a corporate parent, has a responsibility to ensure that young people are being prepared for reviews. Bond and Pickerden (2000) found foster carers had little involvement in such preparation, and in Grimshaw and Sinclair's (1997) study, young people themselves raised concerns about their lack of preparation for review by professionals, and about the adult-focused nature of the review process. Thomas and O'Kane (1998) found children were rarely offered advocacy or independent support at meetings. Other studies, such as that by Hogan and Sinclair (1997), found children and young people living in foster care were less likely to attend reviews than those in residential care. If young people are not encouraged to take part fully in the reviewing process, their opportunities to put forward their views to social services appear to be significantly diminished. Pithouse *et al.* (1994) noted that childcare reviews were typically the responsibility of local area staff and little information was collated for use at central management level. None of the other literature reviewed describes the widespread use of any other alternative route for successfully gathering young people's views about fostering services.

There is awareness in literature that good outcomes for young people depend on young people having a major stake in decision making (Schofield and Thoburn, 1996). Yet in an inspection of fostering services, the Social Services Inspectorate (1996) noted that although children's wishes and feelings were considered, they were not always stated in case records. The Dolphin Project (1993) concluded that involving young people in the development and provision of services may not happen unless someone in management takes on this responsibility, and that this responsibility does not conflict with their other demands. In promoting the Quality Protects Initiative, the Department of Health goes on to state that:

> *Ultimately . . . the real issue is that Councils which fail to consult children are missing out on vital information on the services they deliver and plan.*
> (Department of Health, 2000, p.17)

## Foster carers and problem solving

Foster carers provide young people with family care. They take on a broadly parenting role, yet are temporary carers. The National Standards for Foster Care make it clear that foster carers are 'partners of other professionals in the fostering team' and must operate as part of a team in 'planning and working in the best interests of the child' (Bond and Pickerden, 2000). The professionals within the fostering team typically comprise two types of workers and their immediate line managers: young people's social workers and placement (link) workers (Triseliotis *et al.*, 2000). These workers are therefore the key sources of help and support for foster carers in sorting out problems either for themselves or on behalf of the young people in their care.

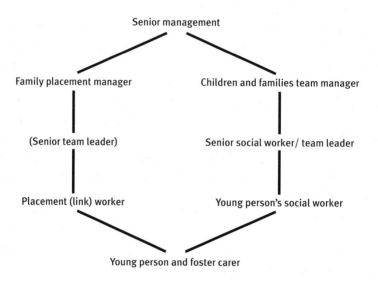

**Diagram 1:  Organisation of local authorities**
Source: Triseliotis *et al.*, 2000

Triseliotis *et al.* (2000) found that local authorities were more likely to define in writing the role of the link worker rather than that of the young person's social worker. Agency manuals usually defined the role of the social worker with children and young people in general terms. Specific guidance on the nature of the professional tasks to be undertaken with young people in foster care was mostly missing. With the split in line management between link workers and social workers, managers in Triseliotis' study described the role delineation of who did what and who was 'in charge' as a grey area. This is likely to cause confusion to foster carers, particularly if, as Triseliotis mentions, there is tension between the social worker and link worker. Managers in the same study referred to a lack of concerted co-ordination and communication between staff, although the ways in which foster carers deal with such tensions is not clear.

Foster carers in Triseloitis' study expressed a greater degree of appreciation towards link workers than to social workers: 88 per cent were consistently satisfied with their link worker, compared with 68 per cent satisfied with their social worker. Where carers voiced satisfaction with link workers this was related to: link workers being available and responsive; their having an in-depth understanding of fostering issues; continuity; and giving their undivided attention to carers. Where dissatisfaction with social workers was voiced, this related to: social workers' infrequent visits and unavailability; failure to provide sustained work with young people; failure to provide sufficient information on the young person's background; and poor overall support. Some managers interviewed were surprised that foster carers had not expressed higher levels of dissatisfaction with social workers' activities, quoting shortages of resources and the many emergency or child protection demands on social workers' time (Triseliotis *et al.*, 2000).

Managers and foster carers in the same study commented on social workers' general lack of fostering experience. Social workers were not always knowledgeable about matters relevant to fostering. They were seen as monitors rather than as undertaking direct work with the young people. Berridge (1997), in his review of research into foster care, reported that social workers in long-term foster care very much responded to issues in placement rather than being proactive. Visiting therefore tended to be a reaction to a problem rather than routine. As a consequence, foster carers were often isolated from social workers. They were reluctant to contact agencies with problems in case this was mistakenly perceived as a sign of being unable to cope (Berridge, 1997). Berridge and Cleaver (1987) studied ten placements in detail. When foster carers were asked who they would first contact concerning serious childcare problems, the majority said they would initially seek guidance from other foster carers or their extended family, rather than the social worker. Regular support of foster households was low on the list of priorities of most social workers. Social workers often stated they felt uneasy when visiting foster homes, suspecting that their participation was unwelcome, yet the foster carers interviewed claimed they would have preferred greater social work involvement (Berridge and Cleaver, 1987).

This evidence suggests therefore that: link workers rather than social workers are likely to be the professionals that foster carers rely on most when trying to sort out problems; that some problems may go unsolved; or that finding a resolution may be a prolonged process of negotiation between different workers.

### Foster carers' participation and influence

All the authorities studied by Pithouse *et al.* (1994) viewed it as 'imperative' that foster carers should be involved in service development. Several of the authorities had carers on various working or planning groups, as did about one-fifth of the 32 authorities studied by Triseliotis *et al.* (2000). Triseliotis found no examples where carers were routinely invited to sit as members of children's services planning committees, and managers commented that it was very difficult for carers to influence policy except through reviews. Carers' input was limited to reviews, occasional groups and directing their views through their link worker. Others commented that carers were not interested in contributing to policy making or did not have the time, or both (Triseliotis *et al.*, 2000).

In the same study foster carers reported a number of shortcomings that service and senior managers were not totally aware of, including social workers' lack of support to some children in foster care and their carers, as well as problems related to payments and conditions of service for carers. Foster carers were uncertain about their role and their relationship with higher management, although they knew that senior social workers were meant to be present at reviews. This was where carers mostly came in touch with more senior management. Carers were mostly satisfied with the way reviews were conducted and with their own contribution, but a minority felt their views were not listened to or valued.

Waterhouse (1997) looked at the participation of foster carers in terms of the proportion of local authorities in England that regularly involved their carers in a number of activities. The results indicate that many authorities routinely involve carers in activities such as recruitment, training, approval and support of other carers, but that carers' input into strategic planning activities or planning for children is limited. When asked about the worst aspects of fostering, the 707 carers in Triseliotis' study placed the operation of the fostering service at the top of their list. Working directly with link workers, social workers and young people, foster carers are in a unique position to inform management about the delivery of their fostering services. As Triseliotis' study demonstrates, foster carers have very constructive views to offer, but consultation with them is mainly at the informal level, between link workers and carers.

## The complaints procedure

The Representations and Complaints Procedure enables children, young people and adults to raise concerns about children's services. As such it can be seen as both a tool for problem solving and a child protection safeguard. Pithouse *et al.* (1994) reported that the complaints procedure was rarely used in foster care by either young people or their carers. Existing research also indicates that young people are less likely to make complaints than adults (Connolly, 1996). This raises the questions about how aware young people are of the complaints procedure. Previous reports of young people's awareness vary. Early studies which looked at young people's experience of making a formal complaint found none of the young people interviewed knew that the complaints procedure existed before the issue they wanted to complain about occurred (Dalrymple and Payne, 1994). Other surveys of young people in care have found that around 80 per cent of young people know how to go about making a formal complaint (Fletcher, 1993; Lynes and Goddard, 1995; Sinclair and Gibbs, 1996). Fletcher's study, though, highlighted the disparity of awareness between different types of local authority care, with those in foster care far less likely to be aware of the complaints procedure compared with those in residential care. Wallis and Frost (1998) also confirm this view.

There is a limited amount of research on young people's experience of the complaints procedure. The Social Services Inspectorate (1998) found the young people they met had little confidence in the complaints process and felt their concerns were not heard. Kelly and Gilligan (2000) suggest that young people in care, particularly in foster care, may feel so vulnerable because of their care status that they are slow to register complaints, fearing the possible fall-out, and may feel inhibited in looking for help. MacLeod (1997) also comments that children do not usually formulate their problems or grievances as a complaint – they simply ask for help.

Wallis and Frost (1998) explored the views of ten young people in foster care about the complaints procedure. They found the young people had particular concerns regarding the consequences of complaining, especially fears that they might be moved. The fear of residential care was a very prominent issue among those interviewed, particularly those below the age of 15. Loyalty and obligation to foster carers were also issues that Wallis and Frost found might hinder young people wishing to complain about standards of care. They report that young people who had formerly been in foster care emphasised the impact that relationships with foster carers had on their ability to complain. Those with positive relationships found complaining had been easier in foster care as they had the support of their carers, but those with negative relationships had found it easier to complain in residential care.

Young people in foster care are far more isolated than their counterparts in residential care, and lack the range of information and support available in some residential units. Their only immediate source of support comes from their foster carers (Wallis and Frost, 1998). Wallis and Frost found foster carers had been given information about how the procedure worked, but social workers had not always discussed the process with them. When considering complaining themselves or on behalf of the children in their care, foster carers tended to see the complaints procedure as a last resort (Wallis and Frost, 1998). The Dolphin Project (1993) found the complaints procedure made many carers anxious. Their main concern was that complaints would be made against them. The amount of knowledge foster carers have, and their attitudes towards the complaints procedure, will inevitably have an impact on young people's access to the procedure and the choices they make about raising concerns in foster care.

Following publicised scandals of abuse in local authority care, both Utting (1997) and Waterhouse (2000) stressed the importance of young people's access and use of the complaints procedure. Waterhouse concluded that:

> *Young people's lack of ability to voice their concerns, or knowledge how to voice concerns, played a major part in the scandal of abuse within North Wales children's homes and foster placements.* (Waterhouse, 2000)

Bond and Pickerden (2000) stressed that all local authorities must develop clearly defined and widely publicised complaints procedures that are truly accessible to all children and young people. However, MacLeod (1996) notes that the 484 young people from foster care calling Childline in the year to March 1996 clearly did not sufficiently trust the adults they knew to discuss their problems and concerns. The report comments that if children themselves do not feel able to confide in adults, safeguards (such as the complaints procedure) – however carefully constructed – will not succeed.

# 2

# METHODOLOGY

*Most literature focuses on specialist or professional foster care despite the fact that this involves small numbers of children and young people* (Berridge, 1997)

## Introduction

Fostering is a public service that takes place in the privacy of people's homes. Any study of foster care relies heavily on the willingness of young people and their carers to talk honestly and openly about themselves. It also relies on the willingness of social services departments to open up their work to close scrutiny. The research it involves can be intrusive and challenging, and these considerations have been foremost in the planning and preparation of this study.

## Planning

Several months were spent in negotiation with each of the three participating local authorities, meeting with senior managers, social work managers, fostering teams, foster carers and young people. Detailed research agreements were drawn up with each authority, including statements on confidentiality and ethics (*see* box right).

Prior to sampling, a flyer about the research was sent to all foster placements in each authority. Short articles were also written for internal newsletters to inform staff and foster carers.

## Question design

Young people, foster carers, social workers and link workers were involved in drafting the interview schedules used. Separate interview schedules were devised for young people, carers, social workers and link workers, each requiring a combination of quantitative and qualitative responses. These were piloted with four foster carers, five young people (aged between 10 and 18 years) and written feedback was gathered from three social workers and four link workers.

A single interview schedule was designed to cater for young people aged eight to 18. All young people were interviewed face to face, and the skills of the researchers were relied upon to deliver the questions in an age/ability-appropriate manner. Interviews with young people were planned to last no longer than 45 minutes.

---

## Research agreement on confidentiality and ethics

The research will be conducted in a manner sensitive to the rights and feelings of those asked to participate. Participation is entirely voluntary. There will be no manner of pressure exerted. To attract participation, the use of token incentive gifts as a gesture of thanks may be used for children and young people.

All information and comments gathered by the research team will be recorded anonymously. The identity of individual participants will remain confidential to the project and those local authority officers charged with negotiating access to voluntary participants. The collection and use of any data in connection with the research relating to individuals shall be treated as confidential at all times:

- All data collected will be maintained anonymously.

- Adequate security measures will be maintained to safeguard such data or material (including tape recording) from access, copying, manipulation or use by any unauthorised person.

- Periodic reviews will be undertaken of the need to retain such data.

- Confidential material no longer needed for research purposes will be returned to source or destroyed.

Should the research team have any concerns whatsoever about the safety of any young person participating in the study, action will be taken in accordance with The Children's Society Child Protection Policy, a copy of which is provided to each partner local authority.

All young people participating in the study will have the opportunity to be interviewed by a person of the same gender and in the presence of somebody else if they wish. All transcripts, notes and audiotapes will be shared with the young people so they are fully aware of the information collected.

Young people who have speech or language difficulties will be assisted to participate. Activities/interviews will be devised to accommodate young people's needs. The research team will endeavour to support the needs of young people whose first language is not English, through the skills of either the project members, the local authority or the child's family and friends.

---

The schedules were designed as the basis for semi-structured interviews. Questions sought:

- To understand the strategies young people and carers might use in sorting out a range of problems that could arise in foster care. Short, fictitious scenarios were used, six reflecting problems young people might come across and six reflecting problems that carers might encounter. The young people's scenarios were put to the young people themselves, their foster carers and social workers. The carers' scenarios were put to foster carers and link workers. This methodology sought to compare the comments made by each group; to understand how young people and carers problem solve, who people talk to, what action they might take, and who else they might involve. Of particular interest was whether carers acted differently when addressing a problem raised by a young person, compared with problems identified by themselves.

- To gauge understanding and perceptions of the complaints procedure – how much people knew about it; whether they had ever thought of using it; what explanations they had for why the procedure was so rarely used in foster care.

- To gauge people's understanding of how young people's and carers' views were fed back to social services managers and what influence they felt these views had on management decisions.

The design of questions put to senior managers was left until all other interviews had been completed. Managers' views had particular relevance to the understanding of feedback systems and the influence of young people's and foster carers' views.

## Sampling

### Young people

A sample target of 60 young people and their carers (20 from each authority) was judged to be both feasible within timescale and financial restraints, and sufficient to produce credible data. We wished to compare the views of different age groups of young people and a decision was made to set the lower age limit at eight years. The local authorities varied in organisational structure, particularly in the way they divided children's services by age group. For the purposes of this study we chose to group together young people aged 8 to 12 years and those aged 13 years and over.

Local authorities were asked to provide lists of young people in foster care aged between 8 and 18 years on 1 September 1999. They were asked to exclude young people in specialist placements and those for whom it was felt the research could prove particularly disruptive or intrusive. As previous studies on foster care tended to focus on specialist placements, it was felt important to draw the sample group from the majority 'mainstream' or non-specialist placements. Allowing social workers discretion as to the names to be put forward was an attempt to honour the ethic that research should do no harm. Purposive sampling was used in order to produce a balance of age, gender and ethnic origin. Twenty-five per cent of all young people written to were from Black, Asian or dual-heritage backgrounds.

Repeated sampling was necessary to attract sufficient participants. Altogether 200 foster families were written to. As an incentive, and as acknowledgement of their time and effort, a £10 gift voucher was offered to all young people who took part. Letters giving information about the research and asking for support were also sent to each young person's social worker. We aimed to interview both the young person and their foster carer. It was important that the views of young people and of carers gathered in the study related to each other. It was clear from conversations with foster carers that many had offered support and encouragement to young people to participate. Without this support it is unlikely that we would have reached our sample target of 60 young people. It is recognised, however, that this supportive relationship will have an influence on the data collected. Participation for young people and foster carers was entirely voluntary and therefore, those lacking support, confidence or interest are not represented.

A balance of gender, age and ethnic origin was achieved, with 61 young people interviewed in all (*see* Tables 1–6 for a profile of the young people's sample group). In 14 cases more than one young person living with an individual foster carer was interviewed and in seven cases only the foster carer within the household took part, the young person having chosen on the day not to participate or having moved since sampling.

There was considerable variation in the length of time young people had lived with their current foster carers. A quarter of young people had moved within the past year. A third of young people had lived with the same family for more than four years. Young people of full African-Caribbean or Asian descent were all living in same-race placements.

Most young people had experienced changes in their social worker during their time in care. About a quarter reported continuity of over two years with the same social worker. Half reported a change in social worker within the past 12 months. About 70 per cent of young people had a social worker of the same gender. Those who did not were predominately boys. Nine out of ten black young people did not have a social worker from a similar racial background.

**Table 1:  Gender distribution of young people interviewed in each participating local authority**

| Local authority | Young people | | Total |
|---|---|---|---|
| | Male | Female | |
| LA 1 | 8 | 9 | 17 |
| LA 2 | 9 | 12 | 21 |
| LA 3 | 13 | 10 | 23 |
| Total | 30 (49%) | 31 (51%) | 61 (100%) |

**Table 2:  Age group of young people interviewed in each participating local authority**

| Local authority | Young people | | Total |
|---|---|---|---|
| | Aged 8–12 yrs | Aged 13–18 yrs | |
| LA 1 | 9 | 8 | 17 |
| LA 2 | 12 | 9 | 21 |
| LA 3 | 11 | 12 | 23 |
| Total | 32 (52.5%) | 29 (47.5%) | 61 (100%) |

Table 3: Ethnic origin of young people interviewed in each participating local authority

| Local authority | Young people | | Total |
|---|---|---|---|
| | White British | Other ethnic origin | |
| LA 1 | 15 | 2 | 17 |
| LA 2 | 17 | 4 | 21 |
| LA 3 | 19 | 4 | 23 |
| Total | 51 (83.5%) | 10 (16.5%) | 61 (100%) |

Table 4: Length of time young people had lived with current foster carers

| Length of time living with current foster carers | Local authority | | | Total (n=60) |
|---|---|---|---|---|
| | LA 1 | LA 2 | LA 3 | |
| Under 12 months | 5 | 7 | 3 | 15 (25.0%) |
| 13 to 24 months | 0 | 5 | 4 | 9 (15.0%) |
| 2 years to 4 years | 7 | 4 | 5 | 16 (26.7%) |
| Over 4 years | 5 | 4 | 11 | 20 (33.3%) |
| Total | 17 | 20 | 23 | 60 (100.0%) |

No response to this question: 1

Table 5: Length of time young people have been with current allocated social worker

| Time with current social worker | Numbers of young people | Percentage of total (n=61) |
|---|---|---|
| No social worker | 1 | 1.5% |
| Less than 1 year | 30 | 50% |
| 1 to 2 years | 7 | 11.5% |
| Over 2 years | 14 | 23% |
| Don't know | 9 | 14% |
| Total | 61 | 100% |

Table 6: Gender of social worker compared with gender of young person

| Gender of current social worker | Young people | | Total |
|---|---|---|---|
| | Male | Female | |
| Male | 11 | 2 | 13 |
| Female | 16 | 29 | 45 |
| No response | 3 | 0 | 3 |
| Total | 30 | 31 | 61 |

## Foster carers

Fifty-six foster carers were interviewed. The vast majority were very experienced. Over 75 per cent had fostered for more than five years and a substantial number for more than 15 years. It is likely that this level of experience and the confidence they had in their own abilities as carers were contributing factors in their willingness to participate. Only eight per cent of the sample group had been approved as foster carers for less than two years. Clearly this will have influence on the data collected. To put this into context, in Scotland 52 per cent of all carers had fostered for less than five years, compared with 26 per cent who had fostered for ten years or more. No comparable English figures are available (Triseliotis *et al.*, 2000). A summary of foster carers' experience is given below.

Table 7:  Foster carers' years of fostering experience

| Length of time as a foster carer | Percentage response (n=56) |
| --- | --- |
| Less than 2 years | 8% |
| 2 to 5 years | 12% |
| 5 to 10 years | 32% |
| 10 to 15 years | 18% |
| More than 15 years | 27% |
| Missing data | 3% |
| Total | 100% |

None of the foster carers interviewed in local authority (LA) 1 had less than five years' experience of fostering, although the differences between the local authorities were not statistically significant.

The majority of foster carers in the sample (65 per cent) looked after young people in both age groups studied (i.e. under-13s and teenagers). Only 17 per cent specialised in caring for the younger age group and 18 per cent specialised in caring for teenagers. Again, there were no significant differences between the local authorities. There were, however, differences between the numbers of young people that foster carers looked after in each local authority. Foster carers in LA 3 on average looked after more young people at any one time than those in either LA 1 or LA 2 (*see* Table 8 overleaf).

Interviews with young people and foster carers spanned a period of seven months, all being completed by the end of May 2000.

## Social workers and link workers

With the sample group of young people and their respective foster carers confirmed, social workers for the young people and the foster carers' link workers were identified. Eighteen of the young people's social workers were interviewed (six from each participating local authority). Of this group, 14 social workers were the allocated worker to more than one child in the sample group. Choice was, in practice, determined by availability and willingness to take part in the study. Those

Table 8: Number of young people looked after by foster carers in each local authority

| Number of young people looked after | Response in each local authority | | | Total |
|---|---|---|---|---|
| | LA 1 | LA 2 | LA 3 | |
| One | 7 | 7 | 3 | 17 |
| Two to four | 9 | 11 | 11 | 31 |
| Five or more | 0 | 0 | 5 | 5 |
| Total | 16 | 18 | 19 | 53 |

No response to this question: 3

interviewed varied in their levels of experience. Two social workers had been qualified for less than two years. Five had worked as children and families social workers for between two and five years, and over half had more than five years' experience. In only three cases did young people in foster carer make up the majority of a social worker's caseload. For the majority of social workers interviewed, young people in foster care made up only a small fraction of the young people they worked with. The study by Rowe *et al.* (1984) showed that social workers supervising children and young people in placement had little prior experience of foster care. This observation is reflected in the comments of the social workers taking part in this study.

Eighteen link workers were also interviewed (again, six from each local authority). Twelve of these supported more than one foster carer in the sample. This was particularly notable in LA 2, where the fostering team was small and the support for the sample group of 18 carers in this authority fell to six individual workers. Again, choice was determined by the availability of staff and their willingness to participate. Levels of experience among the link workers interviewed varied. Six had worked in the same or similar posts for less than two years, two had between two and five years' experience, and ten had worked in the same role for more than five years. The majority of link workers interviewed (72 per cent) supported the placements of at least ten young people.

## Managers

Sixteen senior managers (five from two authorities and six from the third) were interviewed. In each of the authorities studied, fostering workers and field social workers had separate management structures, in common with most authorities in England (Waterhouse, 1997). The decision as to which individuals within each authority were interviewed was delayed to take account of the feedback from young people and their carers. It was decided to interview the following officers:

- fostering team manager/ leader
- fostering service manager
- children's services manager (social work)
- head of reviewing team/ reviewing officer
- complaints officer.

As the management structures of each local authority varied, the officers identified above did not necessarily share the same level of seniority within their respective local authorities. Interviews with all social services staff were completed by June 2000.

In total 169 interviews were undertaken over a period of eight months. A summary is given below.

Table 9: Participants in each local authority

| Local authority | Number of participants | | | | |
|---|---|---|---|---|---|
| | Young people | Foster carers | Social workers | Link workers | Managers |
| LA 1 | 17 | 19 | 6 | 6 | 5 |
| LA 2 | 21 | 18 | 6 | 6 | 5 |
| LA 3 | 23 | 19 | 6 | 6 | 6 |
| Total | 61 | 56 | 18 | 18 | 16 |

## Interviews with young people and carers

A team of four researchers interviewed the young people and their carers in their own homes. The team included one Black male, one Black female and two white female researchers. All team members were employees of The Children's Society. Each had several years' experience of interviewing young people and adults in a variety of settings. Consideration was given to the age, gender and ethnic origin of the young people when allocating interviews to team members. A protocol for interviewing was drawn up and researchers undertook specific training before interviews started.

The interviews were conducted privately and in confidence. The level of confidentiality was explained to each participant at the start – only if the researcher felt a child was unsafe would any information be passed on. All interviews were tape-recorded and participants were also asked to complete tick box sections on the question sheets. Completed tapes and question sheets were sealed together and coded anonymously. These were then returned to the project office for transcribing. Where names were used in text, these were altered to ensure anonymity. Once transcribed, all tapes were erased, again to ensure that confidentiality was maintained.

Researchers were warmly received by both the young people and their foster carers, and interviewees showed considerable willingness to answer the questions put to them. The quality and volume of information gathered exceeded expectations.

## Interviews with social workers, link workers and managers

Members of staff interviewed were all extremely co-operative and provided a considerable amount of data. The same researcher conducted all the interviews with social services staff. All interviews were tape-recorded. Tapes and question sheets were sealed together, coded anonymously and returned to the project office for transcribing. Again, any names used were altered to ensure anonymity and tapes were erased once transcribed.

## Analysis

In a small number of cases technical problems resulted in the recordings being unusable. However, in each case, accompanying notes and the tick box responses provided sufficient data to be included in the analysis.

All the dialogue from interviews was explored using the qualitative software package QRS NUD *IST (Rev.4).[†] This programme allows comments to be categorised and emerging themes investigated. Comments relevant to each project aim were coded and collated systematically. The programme allows easy access to specific areas of inquiry and to data specific to the different sample groups. Quantitative responses together with relevant sections of dialogue were coded and entered in database format. This was then analysed using the quantitative software package SPSS. Correlation and levels of significance between data were investigated.

In addressing each of the specific project aims, qualitative data is complemented with numerical and statistical analysis. While statistical data provides an overview of the findings, the depth of meaning behind the numbers can be illustrated only by the words of those who took part. Great care has been taken to do justice to the young people and adults who spoke openly to us about themselves and their work.

## Recommendations

In order to ensure young people and foster carers were consulted throughout the process of this study, the findings were discussed with young people and carers before the final chapter on policy and practice issues was written. Their views and opinions are therefore included in the recommendations.

## Dissemination

A programme of dissemination to young people, foster carers and social services staff was planned in two out of the three participating local authorities. It is hoped that the results of the study will be used by the local authorities to plan improvements in services to young people in foster care. A summary of the research findings was provided to all participants.

[†] Distributed by SCOLARI Sage Publications Software, London

# 3

# AN OVERVIEW OF YOUNG PEOPLE'S CONCERNS AND SUPPORT NETWORKS

*If I have a problem, I talk to people I can trust, like my carers, my social worker and teachers I know.* (Girl, 13)

## Introduction

The way in which young people approach problem solving has much to do with:

- the kinds of problems that concern them
- how well supported they feel generally and
- the people they choose to rely on.

In contrast to the research and literature documenting the experiences of young people in residential care, there is comparatively little research published that focuses on the views of their counterparts in foster care. Studies that do exist suggest that most children and young people in foster care are extremely positive about their foster placements and look to their carers as their primary source of support (Colton, 1989; Rowe *et al.*, 1984; Shaw, 1998). Other studies suggest that young people in foster care are also generally positive about their social workers and that they value their relationships with them (Baldry and Kemmis, 1998; Fletcher, 1993; McTeigue, 1998). This suggests that there is good adult support available to young people in foster care but does not necessarily tell us how young people use this support when trying to sort out problems they experience. Some studies suggest that who young people talk to tends to depend more on their age and how settled they feel, and that teenagers, perhaps, are more likely to confide in friends than in adults (Bond, 1999; Ibidun, 2000; MacLeod, 1997; Morris and Wheatley, 1994).

In this study we explore the kinds of concerns young people currently experience and their general perceptions about their placements in terms of personal support, and we look in detail at who young people say they rely on when they have problems.

## Young people's concerns

The level of concerns and type of problems young people spoke about varied widely among the sample group, though no obvious pattern emerged in relation to either age or gender. Ten per cent of the young people we talked to told us they didn't currently have any real concerns. They were very positive about their foster placements and the support they experienced, commenting, for example:

> *I don't really have any problems.* (Girl, 10)

The remainder of the group talked about a range of situations that concerned them. Most focused on one particular issue, but others listed a number of different things that caused them concern. As a group, the main issue that emerged was concern about the welfare of their birth families and the contact young people had with various family members. Almost half the young people we spoke to mentioned their birth family as a current concern. These ranged from: a wish to be with, or see more of, their parents; parents' behaviour; the health of grandparents (particularly if they were known to have been ill); worry about siblings placed elsewhere; and general feelings about the lack of information about their extended families. Their comments illustrated their lack of control over these situations:

> *My brothers. I'm not allowed to see them at the moment 'cause my mum won't let me see them.* (Girl, 13)

> *I can't live with my mum because she's in hospital.* (Boy, 13)

> *I want to see my grandma but social services never look into it . . . They know I want to see my grandma, I've mentioned it quite a lot to my social worker. Every time she comes I say, 'Have you spoken to my grandma yet?' And she says, 'I have to look into it' . . . Every time.* (Boy, 12)

> *My mum. She's got emphysema and a drink problem and I'm concerned . . . She doesn't turn up to my contacts and if she does she's like . . . drunk then it like gets her upset and then you think that they're gonna spread your contacts out from two weeks to every month or every two months like that. So I don't tell . . . Like I try to tell my mum to stop it and stuff.* (Boy, 11)

The comments young people made confirm the findings of previous research, which highlight young people's preoccupation and identification with their families. These studies concluded that despite many difficulties at home, young people continued to miss and worry about their families when they lived elsewhere (Johnson *et al.*, 1994; MacLeod, 1996; McAuley, 1996; McTeigue, 1998).

Worries about family members they were separated from, together with other issues related to living with a substitute family, made up the majority of the concerns young people expressed. Two young people had very real anxieties about the permanency of their current placements, even though they knew there were no plans for them to move again:

> *Staying here until I'm 18. That's the most important thing.* (Girl, 13)

Rowe (1984) suggests that, in these circumstances, children are much more likely to see social services as a threat than a source of help and support. They are aware that social services have the power to 'take you away' whether you want to go or not.

The young people we spoke to also expressed concerns that many young people of their age might experience, such as anxieties over their long-term future, school or college exams and career prospects:

> *We're doing GCSEs in May . . . I'm concerned because I'm not too good at school really.* (Girl, 16)

> *My future . . . I might not get a job because I go to a special school.* (Boy, 14)

Although most young people are likely to express anxieties and concerns about their performance at school, these are bound to be exaggerated for young people in care. We know that looked after young people are less likely to achieve well academically. Any move into or within the looked after system is bound to have an impact on young people's education, even when they are able to stay at the same school. Our study revealed that a quarter of the 61 young people we spoke with had moved placements within the past year.

Young people also talked to us about their social life and friendships. Again, although such concerns are relevant to most young people, moving into or between placements clearly puts young people in foster care at a disadvantage in maintaining friendships:

> *[I'm concerned about] my social life . . . I've only just moved here . . . I've got a lot of friends but only a handful live in this area and I don't know my way about.* (Boy, 14)

In the table below responses about current concerns are categorised into those issues particularly relevant to young people in foster care and concerns likely to be relevant to most young people of a similar age. The figures below represent the percentage of the sample group giving each response; therefore no total is given.

**Table 10: Issues currently concerning young people in foster care**

| Issue of concern for young people in foster care | | Percentage of sample group (n=61) |
|---|---|---|
| No current concerns | | 10% |
| Issues relevant to foster care | Concern about and contact with birth family | 48% |
| | Relationships in foster home | 5% |
| | Leaving care | 5% |
| | Fear about being moved | 3% |
| | Safety restrictions | 3% |
| | Past experiences (e.g. abuse/ criminal activity) | 3% |
| Issues relevant to most young people | School/ college/ exams | 21% |
| | Social life/ friends | 12% |
| | Future career | 7% |
| | Own health (smoking) | 2% |
| | Pocket money | 2% |

## Young people's perceptions about their placements

Perceptions about current placements were gauged by asking the young people to agree or disagree with particular statements. Percentage responses are given in the table below.

Table 11: Perceptions of young people about their placement, support and problem solving

| Statement | Percentage response from young people | | | Total (n=61) |
|---|---|---|---|---|
| | Agree | Uncertain | Disagree | |
| Most of the time I am happy where I'm living | 97% | 0 | 3% | 100% |
| There is always someone I can talk to if I have a problem | 95% | 2% | 3% | 100% |
| If I was unhappy I would usually tell someone | 85% | 12% | 3% | 100% |
| Most of the time my problems get sorted out OK | 85% | 2% | 13% | 100% |
| If I have a problem I can sort it out myself | 23% | 38% | 39% | 100% |

The large majority of young people in our study were very positive about their foster placements. At least 85 per cent said they were happy where they lived, they had someone they could talk to if they needed to and they were generally happy with the way their problems were sorted out. Comments such as these were typical of a large number of responses:

> *I've never really been unhappy here.* (Boy, 12)

> *That's true . . . There's always someone I can talk to if I have a problem.* (Boy, 12)

But there was a small group of young people who were not so positive. Two young people out of our sample group of 61 said they were not happy where they were living. Three said they did not always have someone to talk to. Nine (about 15 per cent) were unsure about telling someone if they were unhappy and a similar number felt their problems did not get sorted out well. Even young people who were generally happy where they were living said they would not always share their concerns with other people:

> *I just don't talk about some things.* (Boy, 13)

> *I don't usually talk to anyone.* (Boy, 12)

It was difficult to identify the characteristics of this dissatisfied group. We found no correlation regarding age, gender or the length of their relationships with foster carers or social workers. Girls and boys who had recently moved or who had recently changed social workers were just as likely to feel supported as young people with established relationships. Equally, we found that experiencing longer relationships did not necessarily mean that young people felt any better supported.

## Who young people rely on

In terms of problem solving, some of the young people we spoke to talked about their own resourcefulness, but most doubted their ability to sort out problems by themselves. They looked to the people around them for both practical and emotional support. Some mentioned a fairly broad range of people they might talk to including carers, social workers, siblings, their own families, teachers and friends. But most young people mentioned only a small number of people they trusted. One young girl told us she confided in her 'teddy' a great deal. Another used a notebook to write down her feelings which she later discussed with her social worker. Common responses included:

> *I talk to my foster mum . . . because she helps me through it.* (Boy, 11)

> *I talk to my social worker or my dad or my [foster] parents.* (Boy, 10)

Unprompted, 48 young people (nearly 80 per cent) listed their foster carer as someone they could rely on if they had a problem. This increased slightly to 84 per cent when asked specifically about asking their carer for help. Nearly 60 per cent of the sample group said they would choose their foster carer to talk to above anyone else, although the choice of who to rely on sometimes depended on who was available:

> *There's always someone I can talk to if I have a problem . . . Out of all my family [I'd choose] my-step mum . . . because . . . I understand what she says and like I know her . . . [but] I can't always use the phone to ring my mum so it would be Mel [foster mum] because she's here.* (Girl, 12)

Social workers were also frequently mentioned as adults that young people could talk to about their concerns. Nearly half of the sample group included their social worker in their list of people they would turn to and about 70 per cent responded positively when asked specifically if they would ask their social worker for help. But fewer than ten per cent of our sample said they would turn to their social worker as a first choice. In terms of preference, social workers featured less frequently than friends and siblings. Those who did look to their social worker above others made comments such as:

> *I'd probably talk to my social worker . . . She's the one I know most.* (Boy, 16)

Adults from young people's birth family did not feature very frequently in the unprompted lists of possible confidants, but when asked specifically if they would ask their families to help them, about half of the sample group said they would. Again, only ten per cent of young people said birth family adults were the first people they would turn to if they had a problem.

The tables overleaf illustrate the range of choices young people make in deciding who to talk to about problems they may experience. Table 12 shows the frequency with which particular individuals featured on young people's lists. (The 61 young people we spoke with offered 119 responses.) Table 13 documents young people's stated preferences.

Table 12: Individuals young people choose to talk to about their concerns

| Who young people choose to rely on | Frequency of response | Percentage of sample group (n=61) |
|---|---|---|
| Foster carers | 48 | 79% |
| Social workers | 28 | 46% |
| Adult birth family members | 10 | 16% |
| Teachers | 10 | 16% |
| Peers | 7 | 12% |
| Siblings | 5 | 8% |
| Other adults | 5 | 8% |
| Unsure about telling anyone | 4 | 7% |
| Other, e.g. toys, pets, etc. | 1 | 2% |
| Missing data | 1 | 2% |
| Total | 119 | n/a |

Table 13: Who young people prefer to talk to

| Who young people prefer to talk to | No. | Percentage of sample group (n=61) |
|---|---|---|
| Foster carers | 35 | 57% |
| Other young person (siblings/ peers) | 9 | 15% |
| Birth family adults | 6 | 10% |
| Social workers | 5 | 8% |
| Unsure – dependent on the situation | 3 | 5% |
| No response | 3 | 5% |
| Total | 61 | 100% |

As Table 12 demonstrates, four of the young people we spoke to said they were unsure whether they would speak to anyone about their problems. All of these were boys aged between 11 and 14 years. Their attitudes are reflected in the following quotations:

*I just keep it in until it bursts.* (Boy, 13)

BOY, 11 *I don't talk to people.*
INTERVIEWER So if you've got a problem, how would you deal with it?
BOY *Forget about it*
INTERVIEWER You won't tell your social worker?
BOY *No*
INTERVIEWER What about your foster mum?
BOY *I tell her little things*

When pushed to choose just one person they could talk to, one of the boys did say he would speak to his foster carer, but the other three chose a friend rather than any of the adults around them:

> I'd talk to Aaron, because like if it was about my carers then I know I'd have his confidence. (Boy, 14)

Other young people also had doubts about confiding in the adults they lived with or the adults whose job it was to support them. About 15 per cent (nine out of 61 young people) said they were uncertain about approaching their foster carer for help:

> I wouldn't ask my foster carer . . . I don't have that sort of relationship with her. (Girl, 15)

Nearly 30 per cent of the young people said they were unsure about asking their social workers for help. A third of these (six young people) were quite adamant that they would not approach their social worker:

> I don't really know her. I knew most of my other ones quite well . . . but I don't like to talk [to her]. (Boy, 8)

Again it was difficult to identify the characteristics of these disaffected young people. Teenagers were less likely to confide in their social workers than younger children, but results were not statistically significant.

## Summary

We can draw some conclusions from what young people say about their concerns, how well supported they feel and, more specifically, about who they choose to rely on:

- The majority of concerns young people expressed were about being in care. Their most frequent concern was about the welfare of their birth families and how much contact they had with their families.

- Like many young people, those we interviewed also worried about their education and friendships, but for young people in the care system, these problems are likely to be compounded by moves into and between placements.

- We can identify a majority group (about 85 per cent) that feels well supported in foster care. These young people are happy in their placements, share problems, have someone to talk to if they need to and are generally happy with the way their problems are sorted out.

- The young people in the majority well-supported group have very strong bonds with their foster carers, seeing them as their main source of support. They also feel they can rely on their social workers to a large extent and they may seek support from others such as their birth family, friends and teachers.

- We can identify a minority group (up to 15 per cent) that does not feel well supported. This is likely to include a small group of young people who do not readily speak to anyone about their problems (6.5 per cent in this study). But also an additional, fluctuating group of young people who at different times are unsure about sharing their problems, do not always have someone to talk to and are not always confident that their problems will get sorted out well.

■ This minority group of young people does not rely on foster carers or social workers for support in the way that the majority does. But these young people may rely to a greater extent on others such as friends and birth family.

# 4

# YOUNG PEOPLE AND PROBLEM SOLVING

*If your foster parents weren't nice and your social worker didn't listen, who would I go and ask?* (Girl, 13)

## Introduction

To explore further the ways in which young people problem solve, the sample group were presented with six fictitious scenarios and asked how they might deal with these situations themselves, or how they might advise others. These scenarios explored a range of problems that young people might experience in foster care, from domestic situations, contact with friends and family, to disruption in their foster placement and unhappiness. They were intended as prompts to get young people talking about the ways in which they deal with problems themselves. Where young people recognised the stories from their own experience, they were encouraged to speak about their own situations. Alternatively, where the story was unfamiliar, they were encouraged to offer ideas about what they might do in such situations.

The same six scenarios were also put to foster carers and young people's social workers. This gave us the opportunity to compare whether these significant adults shared the views and perceptions of the young people they cared for.

The responses were looked at in terms of the strategies young people said they would adopt or the strategies adults anticipated they might adopt:

- what action young people might take themselves
- who young people would choose to involve in the problem solving *and*
- the expectations young people might have of other people.

In analysing the responses, we were particularly interested in:

- whether young people use different strategies to sort out different problems
- whether young people, foster carers and social workers share similar expectations *and*
- whether the responses to the scenarios, by both young people and adults, support the recognition of a majority well-supported group and a minority group that does not feel well supported in foster care.

## Domestic problems

Young people, foster carers and social workers were asked their opinions about two specific domestic situations:

**JOANNE**

Joanne shares a bedroom with her foster sister Claire and is fed up that Claire borrows clothes without asking.

**ANDREW**

Andrew's foster mum always gives him baked beans which he hates. When he tells her, she just says he should eat what he is given and she can't be making different tea for everyone.

### Young people

Nearly two-thirds of the young people interviewed said they would initially try to sort out these domestic problems themselves. The suggested strategies varied from practical steps such as hiding clothes, talking to the other people involved and the occasional use of aggression:

Joanne scenario

*I'd talk to her, I'd just tell [her] to stop what she's doing.* (Girl, 17)

*Hit them back. Hit them. Yeah if [they] were wearing my clothes.* (Boy, 13)

Andrew scenario

*[Laughing] If he doesn't like it he should just see when his mum goes out – he could shove them in the bin and go, 'Mum, I've ate them'.* (Boy, 11)

If their own efforts had not been successful in trying to sort out these domestic problems, over two-thirds of the young people said they would probably involve their foster carers. Comments included:

Joanne scenario

*She should talk to Claire and if Claire doesn't listen she should talk to whoever she lives with.* (Girl, 15)

Andrew scenario

*I'd keep trying it a few times. If he really doesn't like it, just keep complaining and she'll probably get the picture.* (Boy, 15)

The majority of the young people indicated the choice of food in their foster placements was unlikely to be a problem for them.

*[Laughing] Not happen. Auntie makes nice tea.* (Boy, 12)

None of the young people interviewed mentioned involving social workers in the issue over borrowed clothes. This was seen entirely as something that would be sorted out between the young people and their foster carers. Ten young people (17 per cent) mentioned that they might involve their social worker in sorting out a situation concerning the choice of food:

> *I'd probably say to my social worker, 'Oh, they keep giving me baked beans every night and I don't like them'.* (Girl, 13)

For most young people, domestic problems were seen as things that could be sorted out with the people they lived with. The majority implied a confidence in their own abilities or the support they expected to receive from foster carers, or occasionally their social worker. In contrast to this confident group, nearly 15 per cent of young people commented that they did not know what they would do in the situations put to them. For some, this was because the situation was outside their experience. But for a few, particularly in relation to issues over food, their responses reflected a sense of powerlessness:

> *I don't eat it. So I get sent to bed.* (Boy, 13)

> *That's what my foster parents say. She just goes, 'If you don't want it, just leave it and go upstairs' and I don't have no tea . . . When I'm upstairs I don't know if she's making tea and I come down and they're all eating . . . and she goes, 'You were too late so you have to make your own tea'.* (Boy, 14)

In the first example the boy had lived with his foster carers for more than three years. When he was asked who he would talk to if something concerned him, he replied 'no one' but when encouraged further he said he would probably talk to a school friend. Other responses he gave indicated he would ask his social worker for help sometimes, but this tended to be about acquiring items such as a mobile phone, rather than an expectation of personal support.

In the second example the boy had lived with his foster carers for more than four years. In response to who he would rely on, he mentioned his social worker and birth family, rather than people he lived with. His preference was to ask his birth family for help. This young boy was unlikely to tell an adult if he was unhappy and he lacked confidence that his problems would get sorted out.

In terms of a model identifying a majority well-supported group of young people and a minority unsupported group, these two boys can clearly be defined within the minority group. As Schofield (2000) commented, 'achieving a "secure attachment" is not just to do with staying in the same foster family for a period of time. It is to do with the quality of the care-giving environment and the quality of the relationships which the child establishes with the foster carers' (Schofield, 2000, p.346).

### Foster carers

More than 90 per cent of carers we spoke to felt they had an important role to play in helping young people solve domestic problems. The responses given by foster carers reflected an acceptance that such things could and should be resolved within the household. Some responses focused on practical solutions such as providing lockable space while others focused on relationships and emotions that might be behind particular behaviour:

> *I think you have to sit the children down . . . try and get some negotiation between the two of them or do it via yourself . . . You might have to look at why they're borrowing clothes. Has one child got more than the other . . . are [they] feeling they're not treated the same or they haven't got the same things? So it's a sit down and negotiate, really.* (Foster carer)

Where choice of diet was discussed, the majority of carers interviewed appeared well experienced at serving multiple-choice meals. Like most of the young people interviewed, carers were often adamant that problems over food would not arise:

> *Oh yeah, it's like a café in this house. We all have different things quite a lot of the time you know . . . It's a case of, if they like it they get it, if they don't they don't. Nobody likes sprouts but I keep putting one on their plate every now and then just to tease them!* (Foster carer)

The strategies suggested by foster carers to resolve the domestic situations presented were very similar to the expectations expressed by the young people interviewed. Carers felt the issues required ordinary parenting skills and several commented that their own children argued about possessions and varied in their food preferences as much as the young people they fostered.

## Social workers

Generally, the social workers from each of the authorities studied also felt the domestic situations posed should be resolved within the fostering household. Their responses reflected the expectations and perceptions expressed by both young people and foster carers. The lack of intervention put forward by social workers suggests they perceive the majority of young people in foster care to be well supported by their carers in resolving domestic problems:

> *I'd feel that was something that the foster carer should be doing. If Joanne was particularly vulnerable . . . I'd speak to the foster carers . . . but hopefully it would be resolved within the family unit.* (Social worker)

Social workers would, however, intervene where a young person alerted them to a problem. As young people mentioned above, they were more likely to seek help from their social worker if they felt ignored by their foster carer. Social workers might speak directly to the foster carer in order to pass on young people's concerns and to discuss possible resolutions:

> *I'd try and establish how big an issue it was, the level that it was happening and I would actually talk to the foster carer to get a clear idea about it.* (Social worker)

They might also choose to go via the carer's link worker, if they felt there were issues about the standard of care being offered:

> *In actual fact I would probably go to Fostering and Adoption and see the [link worker] . . . I suppose I'd pass the buck and say, 'Well, you've got the relationship. That's your job. Can you just go and say in a subtle way that baked beans shouldn't be on the menu every teatime.'* (Social worker)

A few social workers also recognised that complaining about domestic issues might indicate more serious concerns and would wish to explore the situation further to make sure:

> *It could be that the child's saying to you, 'Things aren't right here but I don't quite know how to put it, but . . . she keeps giving me things I don't like to eat . . .' It could be more serious and this child's saying, 'I'm not cared about here.'* (Social worker)

Such comments from social workers back up the feelings of powerlessness expressed by a small number of young people. This again supports a model that recognises a majority well-supported group of young people in foster care and a minority unsupported group.

## Contact with friends and family

Two examples of possible contact problems were put to the young people, their foster carers and social workers. One concerned maintaining relationships with friends, and the other related to contact with birth family. Siblings were used in the example, but the scenario also elicited responses about contact with parents and other family members.

**NAZREEN**

When Nazreen moved to her foster parents, she also had to move schools. She has found it very hard to make new friends and really misses her best friend from her old school.

**MARK AND CHRIS**

Mark and Chris are brothers living with foster carers. Their little sister, Michelle, lives with another foster family in the next town. The boys haven't seen Michelle for over a year and really want to see her again.

### Young people

The responses from young people to problems about contact varied depending on whether the issue was about contact with friends or with family. Nearly 60 per cent of young people commented that they would rely primarily on themselves to sort out contact with friends. Young people saw maintaining friendships as important, especially when they had moved. Typical responses included:

*If I miss my old friend at my old school I would ask him over for tea and to sleep over if I had a sleepover at my birthday.* (Boy, 9)

Only about 20 per cent of the young people we spoke to said they would rely on their foster carer, their social worker, or both, to help them keep in contact with friends:

*I'd tell my social worker and my foster carers about it and ask if I could go and see [my friend] once a week or something like that. Have contact or ring them up or something.* (Girl, 13)

A substantial majority of young people in foster care expressed confidence about keeping in contact with their friends following a move. However, about 15 per cent of those interviewed were unsure what they would do about keeping in touch with old friends. Some had tried and given up, while other young people had no expectations of keeping in contact:

*You ring them and they're not there. It is awful. Like I still remember my friend and haven't spoken to her for two years. I just gave in.* (Girl, 13)

INTERVIEWER  Do you see your old friends?

BOY, 9  *Not 'til I go home when I'm sixteen. I've got seven years left.*

The scenario concerning contact with birth relatives (in particular siblings) elicited different responses. In contrast with maintaining links with friends, fewer than five per cent of young people mentioned that they expected to take the lead in keeping contact with siblings. Over 80 per cent of young people indicated they would rely on their social worker and/or their foster carer, with most young people (about 60 per cent) feeling this was primarily the responsibility of their social worker:

*I'd tell my social worker because she'd be able to sort it out more than my foster parents, I think.* (Girl, 15)

*Ask your social worker to see if they could arrange some time together . . . say every two weeks or something . . . They could have a word with the other social worker.* (Boy, 17)

Some young people reported very positive intervention from their social workers, such as:

*My social worker made sure that my sister came to live here. My foster carer helped as well.* (Girl, 18)

But others had quite different experiences. One 12-year-old girl spoke of her loss of contact with a sister who had been adopted, and her inability to do anything about the situation:

GIRL, 12  *I've had that situation myself. We rang the social workers and we asked if they could find her . . . for my sister to get in touch with me. [My foster carer] was going to try and do something to try*

> *and get her to live with us, but we found out she was adopted so we couldn't . . .*
>
> INTERVIEWER  Would you like to see her?
>
> GIRL  *Yeah, I'll find her when I'm older. I know her first name and that's it. I'll have to go on 'Surprise, Surprise' [television programme] to find her. Cilla Black can find her for me.*
>
> INTERVIEWER  You weren't aware that your sister was going to be adopted?
>
> GIRL  *No, I thought she was fostered.*

Despite her sadness at the loss of contact with her sister, this young girl felt well supported by her foster carer, though angry with social services at the lack of information given to her.

Again, we found a minority group of nearly 15 per cent of young people who were unsure what they would do about contacting siblings, either because this was outside their own experience or, again, because they had low expectations:

> *Well, I went with my brother but I got moved and he didn't . . . I came here and I haven't seen him for ages. I saw him about a year ago.*  (Boy, 9)

This young boy had been living with his current foster carers for less than a year. When asked who he would talk to about problems, he mentioned only his teacher. He said he preferred to try and solve problems alone. He was very clear that he would not rely on his social worker for help. Given his very young age and his perceived lack of support, his comments clearly place him within the minority group of young people who do not feel well supported in their foster placement.

## Foster carers

Where young people had concerns about keeping in contact either with friends or family, foster carers generally saw themselves as the primary instigators in ensuring something was done about it. In contrast to the views expressed by young people, over 85 per cent of foster carers spoke about their central role in helping young people maintain links with friends. It is likely that foster carers are involved to a far greater extent than perhaps the young people acknowledge:

> *Just invite the best friend over. Have a sleepover. See her after school occasionally you know . . . I would encourage them to keep their friends.*  (Foster carer)

Carers seldom mentioned involving the young person's social worker in the issues to do with keeping up friendships, but where they were mentioned, it was for advice rather than any practical assistance:

> *You have to be very careful. Sometimes it is not good for children to see their old friends, as they were a bad influence. I would check with the social worker.*
> (Foster carer)

Most foster carers also expected to be involved in helping young people to stay in contact with their siblings. Where there were no issues of child protection to consider, foster carers said they would expect to liaise with the sibling's foster carer themselves and enable the young people to spend time together. Some carers commented that they would take the primary responsibility. But in common with most young people, the vast majority of foster carers expected social workers to play an active part in keeping in contact, either playing a major role or facilitating initial negotiations and approval:

> *We've had cases where . . . brothers have visited kids at our home. And we've also taken . . . our previous foster lad to see his brother [the other side of the county]. But it's all done via the social workers.* (Foster carer)

Some foster carers talked of their need to be proactive in making sure social workers organised contact between siblings. Where they felt the response from the social worker was insufficient, they were prepared to look beyond that worker:

> *It's really the social worker who knows the background, but you've got to keep repeating yourself. They want to see their sister. Can it be arranged? And if you can't get anywhere with the social worker, then you go to your own link worker or manager . . . but normally it works.* (Foster carer)

Comments made by foster carers about contact with friends and family indicate that, for the majority of young people, both carers and social workers offer good support in maintaining relationships. However, some carers spoke of delays and difficulties in getting a response from social workers, particularly relating to contact with siblings. Such comments again support a model that recognises a minority of young people who are less well supported in foster care.

### Social workers

In maintaining contact with friends and family, most social workers acknowledged the need to be involved at some level. In the case of friends, depending on the relationship with the foster carer and the complexity of the situation, involvement might range from support and encouragement, to close liaison with schools and other individuals:

> *I could get on to the school and find a person who could perhaps take a special interest in her or I might suggest the foster mum just does that.* (Social worker)

The level of social worker involvement was often dependent on how confident or capable they perceived the foster carers to be. Provided there were no child protection concerns, social workers felt established friends should be welcomed to the new placement and effort made by the foster carer (in terms of time, hospitality and transport) to support friendships. This is similar to views expressed by foster carers; however, social workers appeared to accept much greater responsibility in helping young people keep up friendships than either the young people or foster carers reported. Neither the young people nor their carers mentioned the social worker's possible role in liaising with school over friendship issues.

All the social workers interviewed emphasised the importance of keeping contact between siblings, even if there were difficult circumstances and the young people were in conflict. Social workers were clear about the role they would take in addressing the problem. These strategies are illustrated in the example below. If things were working well, they would hope that the foster carers would take over and make arrangements between them. Contact was described as particularly successful where all parties worked together:

> First of all I'd want to know if there were any reasons why the children couldn't see each other . . . I'd be talking to the social worker for the little girl, and the foster carer, and encouraging them to meet, maybe get the carers to meet together somewhere neutral . . . I'd be involved at the beginning trying to get it to happen and then probably leave it to the foster carers if it was working just to keep it going. (Social worker)

Social workers, foster carers and young people all shared the same general expectations where contact between siblings was concerned. However, all the social workers spoke confidently about supporting contact for young people, and did not report on the low expectations expressed by some young people.

## Disruption in the foster family

Young people, foster carers and social workers were asked to consider two different scenarios about disruption in a foster placement:

**LIAM**

Liam has lived with his foster parents for four years. Recently they have started looking after another boy called Tom. Tom often kicks people when he gets mad and Liam is really fed up with this. He spends all his time trying to avoid Tom, and his foster parents seem to have less time for him.

**JENNY**

Living with the Mitchell family has been really difficult for Jenny for lots of reasons. Jenny has been very unhappy at times. She has told her social worker loads of times and said how she felt at meetings. Even Mrs Mitchell told them how bad it got. Jenny often feels like running away. Some days there doesn't seem to be any other choice.

### Young people

The strategies suggested by young people when faced with disruptive situations varied quite considerably. Despite the potential complexity of the problems posed, half the sample group said they would initially try to deal with the situations themselves. They talked about putting up with the difficulties, trying to ignore the situations, or taking some kind of action themselves to change things:

### Liam scenario

*Well if they were getting on my nerves I'd . . . try to ignore him and if he kicks, kick him back.* (Boy, 12)

*We've had lots of kids in the house over the years, so I've got used to it. If you can't learn to live with children that are here, then there's no point in living here yourself really.* (Girl, 16)

### Jenny scenario

*You'd just have to stick with it . . . I just go away from it. Go upstairs or something.* (Boy, 15)

Five young people said they had considered, or might consider, running away if they were particularly unhappy where they were living. Although they didn't think it was a very good idea, it was seen as one way to make people take notice:

*I've ran away a couple of times myself because no one would listen to me . . . Sometimes I feel . . . I'm being pushed out the way . . . There's four kids in this house . . . Linda [foster carer] just sort of . . . shouts at me and she's really kind to them.* (Girl, 12)

But young people recognised that running away did not resolve their problems:

*Well, running away's a bad choice because I've run away a few times because I've had problems . . . I found that just talking to my foster parents, telling them, telling my social worker as well as my foster dad – telling them my problems and my feelings – it works more than just running away from it all.* (Girl, 16)

Where young people spoke of involving adults in trying to sort out their problems, their responses to the two scenarios varied. Half said they would involve their foster carers in a situation where a new child in the household was causing problems for them:

*Talk it through with your foster parents. Tell them you're not happy and see if there's any arrangement you can sort out . . . Ask your foster parents . . . to see if they can do something with you alone without this other lad. Some quality time – just you and your foster parents.* (Boy, 17)

Only about one-third of the group would speak to their social worker about this problem, expecting intervention only if they felt ignored by their foster carers:

*I'd tell my social worker . . . Say that Tom's kicking me and my foster mum isn't doing anything about it.* (Boy, 11)

Two young people mentioned involving their teacher in the Liam scenario, particularly if the kicking carried on at school, and two young people said they would rely mainly on their friends for support if a new foster child was disrupting life at home:

> *I'd tell my friends . . . because sometimes when I tell someone it gets it off my chest.* (Girl, 10)

In the scenario involving Jenny, the young girl particularly unhappy in her placement, less than 15 per cent of young people expected support from their foster carers and only half mentioned relying on their social worker for help and support. Those who did mentioned their social worker spoke about trying to be moved, rather than expecting resolution:

> *Ask her social worker to get her another place if she doesn't like them and they don't like her.* (Girl, 10)

Compared with their response to the previous scenarios, the sample group was far less consistent or confident about how to achieve a positive outcome when presented with disruptive or unhappy situations. Young people who had previously indicated feeling well supported in their placements were at a loss to know who to turn to if expected support was not forthcoming:

> *If your foster parents weren't nice and your social worker didn't listen – who would I go and ask?* (Girl, 13)

There was a sense among many that they did not have many options. One 14-year-old girl mentioned contacting a telephone helpline such as Childline. Four young people said they would turn to birth relatives for support and three (all older teenagers) said they would approach the social work manager if their social worker didn't listen. Only one young person mentioned making a formal complaint:

> *Well, if the social worker isn't doing anything about it I'd go above the social worker and possibly the social worker's manager perhaps, or see another social worker, or I'd place a complaint against the social worker for not doing anything about it.* (Boy, 17)

These responses illustrate that young people's perceptions of being well supported may be fragile and can change, perhaps due to additional pressures on foster carers or lack of attention by social workers. Over one year, the designated Childline number for looked after children received 484 calls from young people in foster care (MacLeod, 1996), giving a stark indication that support for young people in foster care is not always forthcoming. The responses given by the sample group suggests that as well as including young people with persistent poor support, the minority unsupported group also includes those where expected support is temporarily weakened or broken.

### Foster carers

In virtually all the responses to these scenarios, carers spoke primarily about the efforts they would make to change the dynamics in the household. Talking with the child or young person was seen as crucial:

> *I think the foster carer's got to sit down with the child and try and sort something out, because if they don't it's going to break down anyway.* (Foster carer)

> *I've taken a week off work to spend more time and talk to him and the others.* (Foster carer)

Where the disruption was the result of conflict between two young people (i.e. the Liam scenario), carers spoke of the efforts they would make to help the young people understand each other and about practical steps they could take to alleviate the problem. In common with young people, few carers expected the young person's social worker to be involved, unless the situation got out of hand.

Where a young person was clearly unhappy in their placement (i.e. the Jenny scenario), carers were especially concerned to find the cause. Was the young person's unhappiness down to normal teenage anxieties, or past experiences, or was she really feeling unhappy with the people she lived with? Several recognised that moving the young person may not solve the problem:

> *Try and find out why . . . it's not very good to move children round too much because they're not baggage, they're kids, aren't they.* (Foster carer)

In this situation foster carers were far more likely to expect the young person's social worker to be actively involved. Nearly 65 per cent of carers talked about the importance of the social worker's role where a placement was unstable:

> *I would expect the social worker to be doing a lot of work with this child and finding out why she's unhappy.* (Foster carer)

> *Our Sally ran away from us a couple of times . . . we started having family meetings where we all got together . . . with our social worker in as well as the girl's social worker. We didn't want Sally to go at all, but we wanted Sally to be happy. If she wasn't going to be happy with us, then we wanted her to go where she was happy.* (Foster carer)

Surprisingly, foster carers rarely mentioned involving their link worker in sorting out problems presented in the scenarios except in round-table discussions about the dynamics within the foster family. However, where the carer felt they were not getting the response they needed from the social worker, the link worker was seen as the obvious person to contact, as this carer explained:

> *Well, if you're not going to get any help from the social worker, then I would say the link worker, and then after that I would ask to see the link worker's manager.* (Foster carer)

Foster carers' responses to these scenarios differ quite considerably from the comments made by the young people. Whereas young people indicated confusion and a sense of disempowerment in an unhappy situation, most foster carers reported taking on considerable responsibility in trying to improve the situation for everyone. Unlike the young people's responses, foster carers' comments portrayed a confidence that a resolution could be found to relationship problems.

### Social workers

The social workers interviewed shared a clear approach to the scenarios presented on disruption in foster placements, but were not always confident about the possibility of achieving a positive outcome. In common with the views expressed by foster carers, most social workers saw relationships between young people as something that foster carers would try to resolve, probably with the support of their link worker. But social workers expected to play a role to some degree, even if this was simply being kept informed. They would get involved to a greater extent if they felt placements were threatened or if foster carers weren't receiving adequate support from elsewhere:

> *It's something I would expect to be talked about between the social worker and the foster carer. I'd be wanting to understand from Tom why he's behaving like this . . . and seeing how the foster carer is managing and what she's doing about it.* (Social worker)

> *I can think of some families where the level of support from the Fostering Unit is not as good as others, and I think you can tell very, very quickly whether they're getting the support they need as a family. I think that's something that makes quite a significant difference.* (Social worker)

Social workers saw their role as primarily liaising between parties and discussing the issues to try to find the root cause. Where the situation was seen as unresolvable, the social workers saw protecting the established placement as a priority:

> *The child that had been there the longest, I think his needs were seen as paramount . . . There was a meeting . . . and we decided that the other child actually had to move on.* (Social worker)

These comments from social workers contrast with the expectations expressed by the young people interviewed. Less than one-third of young people said they would speak to their social worker about problems with another child in the home.

Where a young person was particularly unhappy in a placement, social workers stressed the need to work very hard to improve the situation and try to understand the cause of the young person's unhappiness:

> *You would try and speak to the young person and find out why they're unhappy . . . What specific things do they think are making them unhappy . . . Then you*

*can work on those things and you can maybe . . . get some support and resources from other areas . . . You've just got to chip away and support the foster carers.* (Social worker)

This reflects many of the responses given by foster carers, although, as demonstrated earlier, young people had much less confidence that such unhappiness could be resolved by either foster carers or social workers. Social workers tended to share the concerns expressed by the foster carers about moving young people on again:

*At what point do you actually give up on the placement and look for an alternative, which may not be any better?* (Social worker)

Social workers were far more candid about the lack of placement choice and whether, in reality, there would be an alternative available. In this respect their comments reflect the lack of optimism in adult intervention expressed by young people. Those young people who mentioned seeking help from their social workers expected to be moved, perhaps with little awareness of the lack of alternatives available:

*In terms of placements, we're absolutely stuffed. If a child goes to a placement that you're pleased with, it's more luck than judgement . . . [This] child is twelve and we need to make permanent plans for her . . . It's just a complete joke . . . You're lucky to have anywhere at all let alone looking for a long-term carer for a twelve-year-old.* (Social worker)

Other studies, such as that by Berridge and Cleaver (1987), conclude that children are frequently placed where there is a vacancy rather than in a household carefully assessed to meet their needs. Comments such as those quoted from social workers in this study suggest that, over a decade later, little progress has been made. The recognition that some young people are placed in less than satisfactory placements again supports the model of an unsupported group of young people in foster care – where carers do not always provide the level of support young people need.

## What works and what doesn't work in problem solving

Responses to the scenarios by young people, foster carers and social workers, together with the findings of the previous chapter, demonstrate that the majority of young people in foster care feel well supported in their placement and have confidence in the adults supporting them. This confidence was explored further, looking specifically at the factors that contribute to good support and also the factors that hinder problem solving.

The majority of young people showed a very clear understanding of the strategies that helped them deal with their own problems. Foster carers and social workers were also very clear about what helped and hindered problem solving for young people.

Young people identified good dialogue, primarily with their foster carers, as the most important strategy in successful problem solving, but they also valued their friends and taking time out to think things through for themselves:

> *I tell Janine [foster carer] and then . . . my social worker comes. She speaks to me, she speaks to Janine, she speaks to everybody in the house and we all try and sort it out.* (Girl, 12)

> *Sometimes . . . I just walk out of the house for a while.* (Boy, 14)

Young people identified being ignored by adults or having their concerns minimised as the factor that most hindered problem solving:

> *Sometimes . . . social workers assume that it's one problem and you try telling them that it's not and that it's something else, but they carry on with what they originally think because they think they're right.* (Boy, 17)

> *Having people ignore me when I'm talking to them . . . My social worker does it if she doesn't want to listen . . . Sometimes my [foster] mum does it as well.* (Girl, 10)

Young people also blamed themselves for adults' reluctance to support them. They were clearly aware of the negative consequences of their own behaviour, whether this was because of their own aggression or anger, or because they bottled up their feelings:

> *I try to sort it out myself . . . I get upset and I start to chuck my fists around . . . It just gets me angrier and angrier and then I get into trouble and then I get grounded and I'm not allowed to go out with my friends.* (Boy, 11)

> *Things like getting into trouble at school and getting into trouble with the police . . . Then it just makes matters worse and then you've got more things to sort out.* (Girl, 13)

In talking to foster carers about what helped and hindered problem solving for young people, two consistent themes emerged: the commitment of the foster carers; and the importance of the young person's social worker:

> *You have to be resourceful and come up with . . . strategies that you would never think of within a family . . . You learn as you go along.* (Foster carer)

> *We had a young girl . . . when she came to us she was the most violent, aggressive and nasty person you could ever come across. She didn't like being the way she was . . . We worked really, really hard, so did she and in the end . . . it was a success.* (Foster carer)

> *He'd been going out and stopping out and going with friends all over the place and we couldn't talk to him and get through to him . . . So we got the social worker . . . and we sat down and talked about it.* (Foster carer)

Foster carers were generally positive about the interventions of social workers, but where problem solving was hindered they highlighted poor social work intervention as the key stumbling block:

> *Sometimes we have social workers not actually thinking about what they've said to children . . . [The children] come back to us and we have to deal with what's been said. We found that happens a lot and that can really put pressure on placements.* (Foster carer)

Social workers placed good dialogue with young people at the top of their list of positive interventions. They also talked about young people's own resourcefulness and recognised the importance of foster carers' excellent parenting skills:

> *I just wouldn't give up. It took nearly six months for him to trust me, but now I feel we've got a very good relationship. We talk.* (Social worker)

> *I have carers now who are exceptionally good – I mean, really, really on the ball . . . they've taken parental responsibility. They're carers who when they feel that something's not quite right with a young person, they've acted straight away and want something done. They're that excellent, they're just . . . really good carers.* (Social worker)

Social workers listed a wide variety of hindrances, mostly focusing on relationships, either between themselves and the young person, or the complicated interactions between foster carers, young people and birth families:

> *Foster carers [sometimes] have difficulties with . . . birth families. If they see a lot of coming and going and the child being upset . . . that can cause problems. Rochelle kept saying she wanted to have contact with her dad but the foster carers were quite anti . . . It caused quite a lot of conflict with the carers.* (Social worker)

Some social workers highlighted problems when young people are not placed with carers who can meet their needs and others noted that some young people have experienced such distress in their lives that problems can be unresolvable:

> *Some of them are not good carers . . . but because they're a rare resource we put up with things we never should.* (Social worker)

> *We've had kids who, because of their family history, haven't been able to settle very well within a family. That's created problems that have been unresolvable and they're moved on, sadly.* (Social worker)

Tables 14 and 15 (*see* right) summarise the responses given by young people, foster carers and social workers, illustrating the similarities and differences in perceptions of what works and what doesn't in problem solving.

Table 14:  What works in problem solving for young people

| What works in problem solving | | |
|---|---|---|
| YOUNG PEOPLE | FOSTER CARERS | SOCIAL WORKERS |
| • Talking things through with:<br>  – foster carer<br>  – social worker<br>  – other professionals<br>  – birth family<br>  – friends<br>• Relying on self/ looking for distractions/ taking time out/ writing things down<br>• Occasional anger | • Resourcefulness, patience and perseverance of foster carers, including:<br>  – good dialogue with young person<br>  – co-operation with other agencies<br>  – good relationships with school<br>  – good relationships with birth families<br>• Good social work intervention and support, including:<br>  – praise for young people<br>  – listening to young people's views<br>  – good communication<br>  – keeping young people in touch with their families<br>  – speedy provision of services<br>  – speedy provision of permanency for the young person<br>  – providing financial support<br>  – co-operation with other agencies | • Good dialogue with young people<br>• Foster carers' excellent parenting skills<br>• Young people's own personal efforts<br>• Working closely with foster carers<br>• Keeping young people in touch with their families<br>• Good placement choices |

Table 15:  What doesn't work in problem solving for young people

| What doesn't work in problem solving | | |
|---|---|---|
| YOUNG PEOPLE | FOSTER CARERS | SOCIAL WORKERS |
| • Being ignored by foster carers or social workers<br>• Having concerns minimised by adults<br>• Getting angry/ getting into trouble<br>• Bottling up feelings/ feeling bullied or nagged at<br>• Trying to sort things out yourself<br>• Running away<br>• Getting bad advice from friends or family | • Poor social work intervention, including:<br>  – not listening to young people<br>  – not listening to carers<br>  – social workers unavailable when needed<br>  – poor decision making<br>  – poor communication<br>  – poor liaison with schools<br>  – poor co-operation between professionals<br>  – poor arrangements for contact with young people's families<br>  – undermining foster carers on parenting issues<br>  – delays in planning for permanency<br>  – inappropriate placement of young people<br>  – lack of support services<br>• Foster carers' limitations, including:<br>  – lack of experience<br>  – not being able to 'get through' to a child<br>  – losing temper | • Foster carers' poor parenting skills<br>• Not being able to form a relationship with a young person<br>• Poor relationships between foster carers and birth family<br>• Lack of planning for permanency<br>• Placing young people across different cultures<br>• Young people's split loyalties between foster carers and birth family<br>• Foster carers' split loyalties between foster families and birth families<br>• Poor relationships between social workers and link workers |

## Discussion

### Young people

From young people's responses to the scenarios we can see that young people do choose to use different strategies to solve different problems. Depending on the situation, they make clear choices about when to involve others and who to talk to. The majority of young people spoke of their considerable reliance on foster carers and their willingness to seek help from their social worker when needed. But the scenarios also highlighted the sense of isolation experienced by some young people. The responses confirm the findings of the previous chapter and reinforce a model that recognises a majority well-supported group of young people in foster care (about 85 per cent) and a minority unsupported group (about 15 per cent).

Taking both the findings of the previous chapter on who young people choose to rely on (*see* Tables 12 and 13, page 26) and the comments made by young people in this chapter, we can identify a core triangle of support for young people in foster care. This is illustrated in the following diagrams.

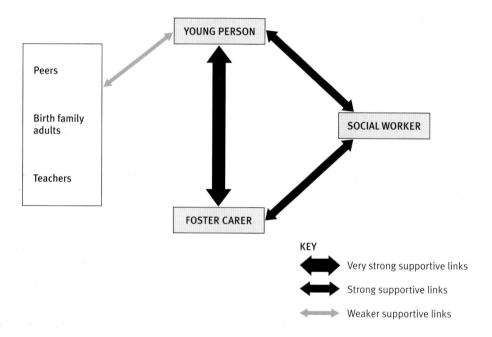

**Diagram 2: Young people's problem solving network – as identified by majority well-supported group**

This core triangle comprises the young person, their carer and their social worker. For the well supported group (Diagram 2 above) we can illustrate young people's expressed reliance on carers by drawing a very strong link between young people and their foster carers. From what young people tell us, this is their most important relationship and has a major influence on how well their problems are resolved.

Strong links can also be drawn between young people and their social workers, based on their expectations of support in relation to contact with siblings and their perception of their social workers as a safety net, should they feel ignored by their foster carers. Young people also expected dialogue to take place between their foster carer and social worker. Many young people expected foster carers to pass on their views to social workers and help in various negotiations. In contrast to this reliance on carers and social workers, this majority group mentioned support from other sources (e.g. birth family, peers and teachers) far less often, therefore these links in Diagram 2 can be illustrated as much weaker.

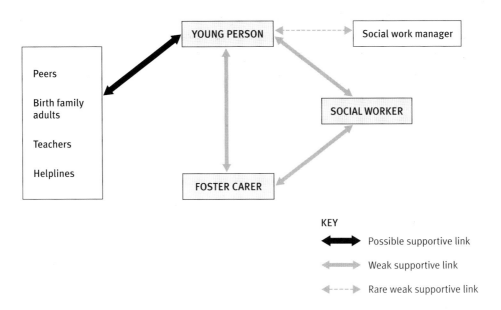

**Diagram 3:  Young people's problem solving network – as identified by minority unsupported group**

For the minority group who do not feel well supported in their foster placement, the link with foster carers (as illustrated in Diagram 3 above) is weak. Up to 15 per cent of young people reported that they were reluctant to ask their foster carers for help and were unlikely to share their concerns with others. When considering what works for young people in terms of problem solving, the lack of good relationships with their foster carer is of major concern.

Young people in the minority group also reported very little reliance on social workers for support. The weaker links throughout this model reflect the sense of powerlessness felt by young people in these circumstances or their lack of experience in being able to resolve problems. These weak links may be a reflection of ongoing poor relationships between the carer, young person and social worker, or may be the consequence of a temporary break in perceived support (for example, where a carer is preoccupied with another child).

If a young person is to receive the level of support experienced by the majority group, other links outside the core triangle will be needed in order to compensate, but this is not what young people reported. There is clearly a need for social services to identify when relationships between carers and young people are failing to provide young people with positive support, and to put in place alternative support. In response to the scenarios, the minority group mentioned reliance on others (for example, friends, teachers, telephone helplines and managers) more frequently than the well supported group. It may be that social services could enable young people's natural allies to be more proactive if other support networks are failing.

## Foster carers

Responses from foster carers confirm the importance of the core triangle of support for young people, i.e. between the young person, their carer and their social worker. The strategies that carers put forward generally reflect young people's expectations and demonstrate their use of different approaches to different problems. Foster carers describe taking a great deal of responsibility in each of the scenarios presented and they are perhaps more involved than some young people acknowledge.

In addition to the core triangle of support, foster carers also recognise a wider problem solving network involving their link workers, liaison with other carers and professionals, and occasional recourse to fostering and social work line managers. Where problems cannot be resolved within the core triangle, foster carers will enlist support from this extended network as depicted in Diagram 4 below.

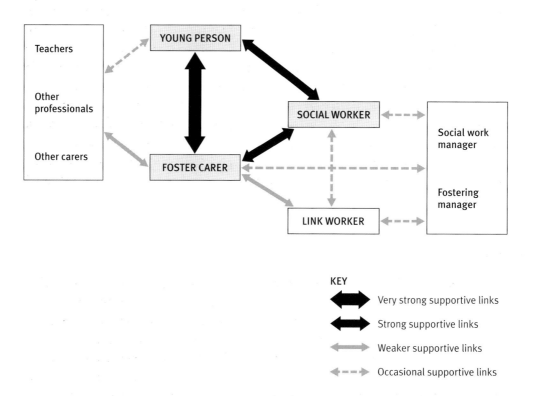

Diagram 4: Young people's problem solving network (majority well-supported group) – as identified by foster carers

As this model illustrates, foster carers' responses to the scenarios showed no recognition of the role that birth families may play in problem solving for young people. Yet ten per cent of the young people interviewed stated that birth family adults were the people from whom they were most likely to seek help. In addition, there is not the same level of recognition by foster carers of the lack of support within the foster home that some young people described. Where carers identify obstacles to problem solving, these tend to focus on poor social work intervention (*see* page 44). In these situations foster carers rely more heavily on link workers and managers in the extended network.

### Social workers

Social workers report that problem solving for young people works best where both they and the foster carers are persistent in their efforts, and committed to the young person. Social workers also acknowledge the skills and strengths of young people themselves. In response to the problem solving scenarios, social workers indicate a confidence that, for the majority of young people in foster care, support within the core triangle works well. This reinforces the model in Diagram 2 on page 46.

Social workers highlight the fact that standards of foster care are variable and that their own involvement fluctuates. Some spoke of the sometimes difficult task of forming trusting relationships with young people, and their perceptions that the relationships between the young person and their foster carers are not always supportive. Such comments provide additional evidence to support the model presented in Diagram 3 on page 47. Most young people are likely to experience some level of diminished support within the core triangle at some time in their foster placement. Despite the efforts of foster carers and social services staff, young people may still regard supportive links as inadequate if problems remain unresolved.

In common with foster carers, social workers also recognise an extended problem solving network similar to that depicted in Diagram 4 on page 48. Social workers, though, see an even more complex picture with further layers of management to refer to. Where supportive links for the young person are weak, especially with the foster carer, social workers will try to engage the help of others in this extended network.

## Conclusion

In this chapter we have identified that most problem solving for young people takes place within a core triangle of support comprising the young person, their foster carer and the social worker. This is a successful model for the well supported majority, but does not meet the needs of the minority unsupported group.

What is clear from the model in Diagram 4 is that young people's access to this wider support network within social services occurs only via their foster carer or social worker. In particular, none of the young people interviewed made any mention of the role the link worker might play in helping to resolve problems for them. If young people feel unsupported by the links within the core triangle (as depicted in Diagram 3) they are unlikely to be either aware of, or able to access, any help from the wider network.

In order to ensure young people in foster care are not left feeling unsupported, social services departments need to focus attention on expanding young people's support networks. This could mean placing greater emphasis on young people's natural allies such as friends and supportive adults outside the core triangle, providing independent services such as advocacy or independent visitors, and ensuring that managers are much more accessible to young people. Developments such as these would offer young people a much broader choice and perhaps greater confidence in seeking support.

## Summary

### Young people

- Most problem solving for young people in foster care takes place within a core triangle of support comprising the young person, their foster carer and the social worker.

- The strategies young people in foster care use to try to sort out problems vary depending on the type of problems they encounter.

- The majority of young people in foster care (about 85 per cent) feel well supported and confident in the adults supporting them.

- A minority group of young people in foster care (up to 15 per cent) do not feel well supported by the adults around them.

- The majority group indicates confidence that domestic problems will be sorted out reasonably well and that any support from foster carers or social workers will be there if needed.

- Up to 15 per cent of young people are unsure about how they might deal with domestic problems. Some within this group feel a sense of powerlessness within the foster household.

- Most young people expect to make their own arrangements to keep in touch with friends from a previous placement or school, but may look for support from foster carers and social workers to help them maintain these links.

- Contact with siblings or other family members are problems that the majority of young people expect their social workers to resolve. The majority of young people express confidence in the help they receive.

- A small minority of young people (between 10 and 15 per cent) have low expectations of maintaining contact with friends and siblings.

- Where young people experience problems with relationships in their foster families they are less confident about achieving positive outcomes, especially if familiar support networks are missing or interrupted.

- Young people identify effective dialogue as the most important factor influencing a supportive relationship.

- Young people identify being ignored, not being listened to or having their concerns minimised by adults as a significant factor in diminishing their expectation of support.

- Young people also identify their own anti-social behaviour and reluctance to share concerns as contributing to diminished support.

- Young people do not have access to the wider support networks within social services identified by foster carers and social workers.

### Foster carers

- Foster carers demonstrate considerable responsibility in trying to sort out problems for young people.

- The strategies foster carers use to help young people problem solve vary depending on the type of problem encountered.

- Foster carers broadly share the same expectations as young people about how to approach specific problems, but are likely to be more involved in problem solving than some young people acknowledge.

- Foster carers acknowledge the importance of the core triangle of support for young people. But they also recognise an extended network including link workers, other carers and professionals, and occasional recourse to fostering and social work line managers.

- Foster carers acknowledge the division of young people into a majority well-supported group and a minority unsupported group. But there is not the same recognition of the lack of support within the foster home that some young people describe.

- The two consistent themes reported by foster carers as contributing to successful problem solving with young people are: the resourcefulness, patience and perseverance of foster carers; and good social work support and intervention.

- Foster carers identify poor social work intervention as the largest single factor that diminishes expectations of successful problem solving.

### Social workers

- Social workers report a wide variation in the amount of problem solving they undertake with young people. This is a view shared by both young people and fosters carers interviewed.

- Social worker involvement in young people's problem solving varies depending on the type of problem and their personal relationship with the young person.

- Social workers generally have similar expectations to those of young people and foster carers in their approach to specific problems. They highlight the importance of the foster carer's role.

- Social workers recognise the division of young people into a majority well-supported group and a minority unsupported group.

- Social workers also recognise an extended support network beyond the core triangle, comprising: the link workers, other carers and professionals, fostering and social work line managers, and senior managers.

- Social workers identify good dialogue with young people and foster carers, and the excellent parenting skills of foster carers, as factors that promote effective problem solving for young people.

- Poor standards of foster care and an inability to engage with some young people are identified by social workers as the main factors hindering problem solving.

# 5

# FOSTER CARERS AND PROBLEM SOLVING

*The only way to get things done is to do it yourself unless you've got an exceptionally good social worker.* (Foster carer)

## Introduction

Having looked at the ways in which young people problem solve and the role played by foster carers, in the following chapter we specifically consider the ways in which foster carers problem solve. Whereas in the previous chapter we focused on situations that young people themselves might raise, here we look at situations foster carers identify, and compare the differences and similarities of their approach.

A series of six scenarios were presented to the sample group, using the same methodology as before. The examples given dealt with a range of problems that foster carers might experience, such as getting information, emergency placements, being consulted, division of roles and responsibilities, social workers' actions and changes of social workers.

The scenarios were intended as prompts to encourage foster carers to speak about their own experiences. The same six scenarios were also put to link workers, giving us the opportunity to compare expectations. We looked at responses in terms of the strategies foster carers said they would adopt or the strategies link workers anticipated they might adopt:

- what action foster carers might take themselves
- who foster carers would choose to involve in the problem solving *and*
- the expectations foster carers might have of other people.

In analysing the responses we were particularly interested in:

- whether foster carers use different strategies to address problems that they themselves identify, compared with problems that young people might identify
- whether foster carers and link workers share similar expectations.

## Information on young people

Foster carers and link workers were asked their opinions about how to resolve the following situation:

> **MR AND MRS JACKSON**
>
> Mr and Mrs Jackson have been looking after Leanne (aged eight) for two months now but have very little information about her or what plans are being made for her.

### Foster carers

Foster carers were well aware of the importance of having accurate information about the young people they looked after, not only to enable practical tasks such as registration with schools and doctors, but also to try and meet the young person's emotional needs. If the information was not forthcoming within the first few days or weeks of a placement, foster carers were prepared to push for the information they needed. Many spoke of 'badgering' or 'getting on at' the social worker repeatedly until they came up with the information. If this was unsuccessful, or was taking too long, foster carers would approach their link worker to enlist their support, or would contact the social work manager directly:

> *I'd contact the child's social worker and if I couldn't get the information I required, I would get my link worker to do it for me and ask for plans . . . I would be shouting quite loudly.* (Foster carer)

> *I would ring [the] social worker . . . to get the information . . . If that didn't happen I would be talking to his or her team leader. I would definitely keep at it until I got what I needed.* (Foster carer)

The amount of information foster carers usually received varied between the carers interviewed. For some, it was commonplace to have sparse information or to persistently have to contact social workers to get information. Most foster carers were generally happy with the amount of information they eventually received. A few voiced acceptance that, for some young people, there was very little known by anyone:

> *These two [young people] I've got, no one seems to know a right lot about their background. I've got bits and bats so I've just had to work with what they've got because nobody seems to know.* (Foster carer)

In getting information that was not easily forthcoming, foster carers stressed the importance of knowing which workers to contact, i.e. who was more likely to pursue matters for them. They felt this knowledge came from experience, rather than from a clear organsational system of contacts. Generally, foster carers expected to receive good-quality information from social workers straight away. Where this didn't happen, they would persist with requests and rely on their link worker or the social worker's manager to help resolve the situation.

### Link workers

Link workers acknowledged that, in emergency situations, the passing on of information was not always given the priority required:

> *The actual placement being made has alleviated the initial anxiety of the social worker and they've gone off to get on with something else. And the foster carer's left feeling, 'What do I do here?'* (Link worker)

Link workers expected a review or planning meeting to be held within the first week or month of a new placement, depending on the local authority. The responsibility for passing on information about a young person was seen to lie primarily with the social worker. Link workers saw their role as liaising between the foster carer and social worker where necessary, supporting the views expressed by carers above.

All of the link workers interviewed said they experienced having to regularly chase social workers for information. Link workers reported making repeated telephone calls to social workers, sending memos or physically retrieving information themselves. If social workers did not respond, link workers would involve line managers to move the situation on:

> *If I didn't get satisfaction . . . I would send a memo . . . to the area manager and it filters back down . . . You haven't got the clout to tell the social worker exactly what to do.* (Link worker)

Some link workers recognised that particularly experienced carers were well skilled in chasing information, and they would only get involved if carers were inexperienced or there were serious blocks in communication. This also reflects the views expressed by foster carers above, where many spoke confidently about pursuing the information they needed themselves.

## Emergency placements

Foster carers and link workers were asked how they would deal with a situation in which the foster carers felt pressurised to accommodate additional young people in an emergency.

**MRS PORTER**

Mrs Porter is registered to foster up to two children long term, but recently has taken in children in an emergency. One week she looked after four children in all. While she feels she can't say no, Mrs Porter is also conscious that the emergencies are unsettling for the two children living with her long term.

### Foster carers

Many of the carers interviewed reported having experienced similar situations. Even if they were registered as long-term carers or their households were already full, they had still felt pressurised to accept additional young people in an emergency.

Pressures came from social workers and, in particular, the emergency duty teams:

*Yeah, I had a baby [placed] five or six weeks ago. When I went long term I gave back all my baby equipment . . . but EDT [emergency duty team] know who they can ask and can't ask. You can always say 'no', but in the early hours of the morning you tend to say 'yes' because you know they're really struggling. It's emotional blackmail really.* (Foster carer)

*It was the social worker who was asking and her boss also begged us. So we did, we had two more kids than we should have done and it was chaos. When our link worker found out she was furious.* (Foster carer)

Some foster carers were clear that they were not obliged to take additional young people and were angry that social services could disregard registration limits and put such pressure on them:

*Don't go outside your registration. It causes problems. They're the ones that go wrong . . . They shouldn't even ask . . . because some people can't say no.* (Foster carer)

But foster carers were aware that, without a large pool of carers, social services had to try and place young people where they could:

*They're not the ideal placements for the child or the family . . . It's just a matter of – put them wherever you can fit them in. A lot of time the planned moves for children don't happen because they're dealing with emergencies. [Then] the planned moves start to get more urgent than they admit.* (Foster carer)

Faced with this situation, foster carers were equally divided between those who would offer help and those who would resist the pressure put on them. Where carers said they would help, most were clear about setting and sticking to specific time limits for the emergency placements. Where the situation became too difficult or unstable foster carers would try to make this clear to the social worker and engage the support of their link worker. The needs of the young people living with them long term were seen as the priority:

*If they are unsettling for the long-term [children] then obviously the priority for us are long-term ones so we put a time limit on emergencies . . . and stick to it.* (Foster carer)

Carers felt resisting pressure was difficult. Even when they knew they were making the right decision for their family, they still experienced a sense of guilt at turning away another young person in difficulty:

*It's very difficult to say 'no' under those circumstances when you have an emergency . . . Where does this kid go? Is it better she comes to you or goes to a kids' home?* (Foster carer)

The foster carers interviewed felt they had learnt to be more assertive with experience. With over 75 per cent of those interviewed having fostered for five years or more, this was a common theme in many of the responses given.

### Link workers

Link workers interviewed all expressed concern and a protective attitude towards their foster carers. There were some, however, who were confident that carers would not be pressurised into taking additional young people. Others hoped the situation would not occur, but knew that sometimes, foster carers did feel under pressure if a child had nowhere to go. Link workers felt it was their role to ensure carers were not overstretched:

> *It is important that we look after foster carers in terms of their time, their health, their sanity really, and also the other children that are in placement . . . We'd have to look at what else we can do in that situation rather than exhaust the people that we've got.* (Link worker)

Common themes in link workers' responses were: encouraging and supporting their carers to say 'no' to additional placements; knowing which of their foster carers could be approached if needed; and the importance of offering good support to the family. If the situation for the carer was getting out of control, the link workers saw it as their responsibility to find a solution, especially if the emergencies were jeopardising long-term placements:

> *If the carer . . . came to me and said, 'Look, I am struggling with this' . . . I would advise her to call an early review or [I'd have] spoken to my manager and looked for alternative placements because the two long-term placements are imperative to keep maintained.* (Link worker)

Both foster carers and link workers recognised the need to protect the family from disruptive emergency placements. Strategies suggested by both were similar, i.e. resisting pressure and saying no to requests, or ensuring good negotiation and clear expectations. While foster carers themselves expressed a level of confidence in managing such pressures, comments from link workers reflected their protectiveness and a sense of 'parental' concern.

## Cancelled meetings

The following scenario looked at the consideration given to foster carers over arrangements for meetings.

**MR JONES**

Mr Jones has to take time off work to attend his foster son's review meetings. The last two have been cancelled at short notice. This causes difficulties for Mr Jones at work, as his manager is not very sympathetic.

## Foster carers

Foster carers gave a variety of responses to this scenario. The majority did not see cancelled meetings as too much of a problem. They acknowledged that if people were ill, for example, meetings had to be cancelled at short notice. But such comments came from carers who were either both at home full time, or where there was one full-time carer who could be flexible:

> *Well, we basically made the choice when we started [fostering] that one would stay at home . . . For the last ten years there have been two of us at home so the situation has never arisen. We wouldn't have gone into fostering if we hadn't have been able to give some form of commitment.* (Foster carer)

> *I would go on my own . . . As long as one's there anyway, I can't see that it should make a difference.* (Foster carer)

But for some foster carers repeated cancellations were seen as unacceptable and did cause problems. Carers, though, were not always sure what they could do about it:

> *It is inconvenient. You make arrangements . . . I struggle sometimes to get the time off and after I've gone to all that bother to . . .you get a telephone call a couple of hours before and it's, 'Oh so and so's gone sick. We can't hold it now.' It does cause problems.* (Foster carer)

Cancellation of arrangements was seen as fairly commonplace. Where it became unacceptable, some carers said they would complain to social workers or link workers, or seek recompense in some way. Many stressed they would ensure meetings were arranged at a convenient time for them, rather than always working to suit social workers. Only three foster carers mentioned that cancellations caused more distress to young people and their families than to themselves, and that it was the young people who should be given greater consideration in such circumstances:

> *I mean, they're more inconvenient for the young people . . . [not] fitting in with school times and work. Social workers will not often work beyond five o'clock . . . my son's . . . at work so he doesn't come home until half past five.* (Foster carer)

Foster carers reported being remarkably flexible and tended to view cancelled meetings as an inevitable hazard of working with social services. Where cancellations were persistent or caused difficulties, they would generally make their needs known to social workers or enlist the help of their link worker.

## Link workers

Link workers were very understanding of the needs of foster carers when it came to planning times for reviews and other meetings. There were repeated comments about the lack of consideration given to carers and recognition of the importance of the main wage earner's employment:

> *I'm pretty sure that everybody else's circumstances are thought about but people*

*just think that foster carers are there. People don't often stop and think if the time is suitable for them. We usually try and say to social workers, 'Speak to the foster carer first . . . see what their availability is.'* (Link worker)

If the timing of meetings was causing problems, link workers saw their role as negotiating between social workers, other professionals and carers, and emphasising the carers' needs. This wasn't always successful, however. If carers couldn't attend a particular meeting, then link workers tried to ensure they attended instead and fed back to carers later. Attempts to negotiate were sometimes frustrating:

*I've just . . . had a huge row over the timing of the review. [It] was set for half past two in the afternoon and the foster carer had to pick up children at three o'clock. Both me and my team leader had a go at the social worker and his team leader about [the timing]. We wanted it cancelled and rescheduled. In the end it still went ahead. My success rate was zilch there . . . The primary carer was not at the review . . . Crazy.* (Link worker)

Each of the local authorities in this study had recently introduced independent reviewing teams. The feedback from link workers was that this introduction had improved planning and there did appear to be more consideration of foster carers' other commitments:

*Now we've got an independent reviewing team they're much better at it than the social workers were.* (Link worker)

Link workers shared foster carers' expectations of their role in sorting out problems with cancelled meetings. However, they appeared to regard cancelled or poorly scheduled meetings as more disruptive and inconvenient to foster carers than foster carers themselves reported.

## Division of responsibilities

The following scenario looked at the division of roles and responsibilities between the foster carer and the social worker.

**MRS AHMED**

Mrs Ahmed has mentioned to Shaheen's social worker twice now that Shaheen might need glasses. The teachers at school don't think she can see the board clearly. Mrs Ahmed is still waiting for an optician's appointment to be made.

### Foster carers

Virtually all the foster carers in our study were clear that they would take responsibility and make an optician's appointment without waiting for a social work decision. All the responses were very similar, stressing carers' expectations that eye tests, dental appointments, etc. were part of their role:

*I'd take them to the optician's myself. I wouldn't wait for the social worker to say that they needed glasses. If I thought that the children were suffering from headaches or that there are concerns at school, you have to handle that as if they're your own children. Inform social services that you're going to do that or that you've already done it. It doesn't really make any difference.* (Foster carer)

*Don't wait for anybody, do it yourself. The only way to get anything done is to do it yourself unless you've got an exceptionally good social worker who just happens to have the time. Things like that I never leave to social workers. I work on the assumption that if you do it for your own child then you do it for foster kids.* (Foster carer)

Only one carer said they would seek approval from the social worker before taking action, stating they wouldn't do anything without the social worker's approval. Confidence to take the initiative, as one carer commented, came with experience. The example below describes how foster carers might well feel restricted in their role or confused over job boundaries:

*They tell you, you have to treat these children like part of your family and then restrict you from doing so. You can't give permission for haircuts; you can't give permission for ear piercing. You just really don't know what you are allowed to do . . . Social workers . . . assume because we have taken on roles over the years that it's our job when, in actual fact, when you read the instructions, it is the social worker's responsibility, but we have . . . to make sure the child gets what it needs.* (Foster carer)

Foster carers reported they would generally consult the social worker if funding was needed for specific items. Otherwise foster carers would sort out issues such as optician's appointments themselves without recourse to others.

## Link workers

The responses given to this scenario were all very consistent. All link workers regarded it as entirely appropriate for foster carers to make this kind of appointment themselves. They expected such roles and responsibilities to have been discussed and sorted out in planning meetings and reviews. As a precautionary measure, a number of link workers said they would check with the social worker to ensure there was no confusion:

*Often the foster carer would just get on and do it themselves . . . There's a huge variation in what foster carers feel able and confident in taking on . . . Sometimes you just need to check [it] out with the social worker . . . But . . . most foster carers that I've worked with would just do it.* (Link worker)

*I think foster carers quite often are better at getting a job done than waiting around for other people to help them do it.* (Link worker)

If Mrs Ahmed did not feel confident, perhaps because of a language barrier, link workers expected the social worker to offer assistance, but would be happy to help out if necessary:

> *Well, I would see it as the foster parent's job . . . If there were language problems then it would either be down to the link worker or the child's social worker . . . to provide an interpreter.* (Link worker)

Link workers and foster carers were both confident that making an appointment at the optician's, for example, was something foster carers would do without the need for assistance. Where help was required in meeting the needs of a specific young person, link workers saw this as the social worker's role. But where there were issues about carers' confidence or the division of responsibilities, link workers would be involved.

## Actions of social workers

This scenario looked at problems that can arise when working with more than one social worker.

**ALISON**

The school trip is in two weeks' time. The eldest of Alison's two foster children has the okay to go, but Mark is still waiting to hear. He is getting very anxious and takes it out on the older boy.

### Foster carers

Again, most of the foster carers interviewed said they would be very persistent in phoning the social worker to get a decision, using phrases such as 'hound', 'pester', 'badger', 'pull the stops out', reflecting their determination to solve the problem. Foster carers might negotiate directly with the school, and several said they would make their own judgement if a response from the social worker was not forthcoming:

> *I'm afraid I would start ranting and raving down the phone at social workers to get the okay. If I didn't get it then I would let him go if it was a school trip.* (Foster carer)

> *I'd get on to the social worker that's slacking and tell them to get their finger out . . . [I'd] let them go and then sort it out. If the social worker shouts at me then I'll shout back.* (Foster carer)

Other foster carers said they would approach line managers and perhaps get their link worker involved. Some strong feelings were expressed about ensuring young people were treated equally:

> *[There's] no difference between kids. They both go and you worry about the cost afterwards . . . Some social workers will say, 'Yes, we'll fund it.' Others say,*

*'I'll have to see my line manager.' I'm afraid that doesn't work in a normal family. You make them all alike. There's no exception to that rule as far as we're concerned.* (Foster carer)

Foster carers recognised the difficulties that can arise working with more than one social worker. Carers commented that this was more noticeable when the young people came from neighbourhoods covered by different area offices. Social workers themselves varied and some practices also varied between one area office and another. The following comment by one foster carer describes the difficulties that this can cause:

*We've often had three lots of [social] workers, three lots of meetings . . . [It's] hard when you get a really good worker and then you get one who just couldn't care less. Because the really good one will come out and do work with that child and do what she has to do. And the other child is just left on a limb. What message does that give them? You're trying to treat them all the same . . . but social workers are a law unto themselves sometimes.* (Foster carer)

Where securing finance was a problem, many foster carers said they would provide the funding from their own resources, sorting it out with social services later, or covering the costs themselves. If there was a specific reason why the young person couldn't go on the trip, foster carers felt it was important to talk this through with the young person and perhaps provide an alternative.

The responses from foster carers here show their considerable determination and persistence. They expected to have to take the lead in trying to speed up a social work decision, involving managers and link workers where needed. Where the problem was not being addressed quickly enough, foster carers might negotiate directly with school and might take decisions themselves, even when this was outside their responsibilities. Common themes in all the responses were: ensuring that young people did not miss out on opportunities because of social work inaction; and trying to ensure all young people were treated equally.

## Link workers

Link workers were well aware that foster carers experienced very variable input from social workers and that this could cause considerable problems in a household with unrelated young people. The comment below reflects the frustrations felt by some link workers about the input of social workers:

*Wouldn't it be nice if you could match the social worker rather than the child . . . There are times when you look through the referral list and you think, 'Oh, so and so would match . . .' and then you look at the social worker and your heart sinks. You know you're going to have your work cut out but you have to go with it. It's the child that matters.* (Link worker)

If obtaining permission for a school trip was a problem for a young person, link workers would expect to be actively involved in trying to sort out the situation – liaising repeatedly between the foster carer, social worker and the school. Some link workers noted that conflicts could arise between social workers and foster carers that make this kind of liaison particularly difficult:

> *A lot of foster parents that have been around [a long time] are very sort of gobby, understandably so. They are looking after the child so they want what's best for that child and I think some social workers find that hard. They feel the child is their responsibility and they have the say. I mean, there are times when you have to sort of sit in the middle of mega-arguments between social workers and foster parents . . . but carers do a really good job and should be supported to the hilt.*
> (Link worker)

Where the link worker felt the social worker was causing delays they would take the issue up with the social work manager. Several link workers said that if they felt delays were simply bureaucratic, they would take responsibility for the decision making themselves. Link workers understood the jealousies that could arise within the foster home where young people experienced different levels of social work or family interventions. Supporting carers in such situations was seen as a key part of their job.

Link workers saw themselves as taking a significant role in liaising with social workers, whereas most carers expressed confidence at being able to deal with social workers directly. Foster carers indicated they were more likely to approach social work managers if they experienced inaction or delays rather than expecting the link worker to resolve the situation. Link workers, however, recognised that the personalities of workers or foster carers could have considerable influence on the situation.

## Changes of social worker

This scenario looked at the disruption caused by repeated changes of social worker.

**LINDA**

Linda is concerned that Sarah, 13, has had three changes of social worker in the last two years and nothing seems to be happening about the long-term plans made for her.

### Foster carers

Many foster carers recognised the disruption that frequent changes of social worker caused for young people:

> *This is something which affected one of my children. He had six social workers in a very short time – he became very agitated and refused to talk to them.*
> (Foster carer)

But others felt that, especially for those in long-term placements, it was the foster carers rather than the social workers who provided the stability young people needed:

> *We've had changes of social workers but in our particular case I think we try and*

*make more of a bond with the child. Although the social worker's important
I don't think they're as important as being a foster carer for the child. I think the
security part comes from you and your child, and the social worker is sort of
secondary to that . . . I find when the social workers come the children tend to
think, 'Oh God, what's happening now?' . . . They just say, 'Hello' and go.
I don't think they want to be bothered with them.* (Foster carer)

The foster carers interviewed suggested various approaches to the problem in the
scenario. They felt they could do little about changes of personnel, but would act if
the changes were causing problems and especially if plans were not being progressed.
Foster carers said they would keep chasing the new social worker and perhaps seek
support from their link worker:

*Again, it's all down to the carer pushing . . . and literally ringing maybe three
times in a week and just keep on their back.* (Foster carer)

*Again I would get in touch with my link worker. Get her to put some pressure on
them.* (Foster carer)

Foster carers suggested calling a review or planning meeting, or complaining to a
social work manager. Some accepted that personnel changes were inevitable but that
they would do their best to reassure young people. A couple of carers found the
question amusing, given that the young people they were caring for didn't even have
a social worker, let alone changes of social worker!:

*Well, she's lucky if she's had three social workers really, because you get kids that
are with you for 18 months and they never see a social worker so I wouldn't
know what to do about three different social workers because once our social
workers leave we never get another.* (Foster carer)

Foster carers again expressed their determination and persistence at trying to resolve a
problem they identified. But as they have little control over changes of social
workers, they sometimes felt powerless to provide the continuity of care young
people need. In this situation, foster carers are likely to rely more on their link
workers and social work managers to ensure childcare plans are made and followed
through, and to minimise the effects of disruption for young people.

### Link workers

Link workers were conscious of the effects frequent changes of social worker could
have on both young people and foster carers:

*I tend to find that this makes foster carers feel very insecure, which is
understandable . . . We take on foster carers and push forward the idea that
they're working as part of a team, only then for . . . it not to happen like that.
Feeling that they're not being consulted. Feeling that they're not being given the
consideration . . .* (Link worker)

If people were clear about plans, and reviews were held regularly, then link workers hoped the chances of plans not happening were minimised. But calling additional meetings was not always easy:

> *Our carers have the right to demand a review . . . I've just done [that] with one carer . . . The social worker wasn't very happy about it, but tough . . . With most social workers . . . we have good working relationships and we work very much as a team, but there are the odd ones that resent our interference, as they see it.*
> (Link worker)

Good communication was seen as key. Problems arose where communication was poor and link workers again emphasised the impact personalities can have on a situation. Link workers would try to improve communication, but if this didn't work they would involve their managers to bring some pressure on the situation:

> *I would talk to the foster carer. I'd be monitoring it. I'd take it back to my manager and get her to speak to [the social worker's] manager. It's not good enough . . . They should have an overall plan and carry something through.*
> (Link worker)

Where there were frequent changes of social worker or perhaps an unallocated social worker, link workers clearly saw their role as trying to maintain continuity for the foster carer. Foster carers shared this expectation. Half of the young people interviewed in this study had changed social workers within the last twelve months, highlighting the need for this continuity. Both link workers and foster carers also recognised the role managers can play in trying to secure continuity of social work and effective planning.

## What works and what doesn't work in problem solving

Foster carers demonstrate very high levels of responsibility in trying to resolve problems. They ranked support from their link workers, and their own experience, as the key elements in sustaining their confidence and skills, for example, regarding their own abilities:

> *I'm usually good at sorting any problem out.* (Foster carer)

> *The problems I have, they're not what I'd call mountainous.* (Foster carer)

Regarding link worker support:

> *She's lovely . . . Really supportive and she's around when you need her . . . You know you're getting backup and support.* (Foster carer)

> *The fostering unit . . . were brilliant. They were supportive. They listened. They appeared to understand.* (Foster carer)

Over 80 per cent of foster carers rated the involvement of both their link workers and young people's social workers highly in helping to resolve problems. Responses to the scenarios by foster carers, though, show that when help is needed for a specific problem, foster carers rely to a greater extent on young people's social workers. They spoke of involving link workers (or managers) only if the help they expected from social workers was not forthcoming. But compared to carers' responses in Chapter 4, foster carers mention reliance on link workers more often where they themselves identify a problem, than when a young person raised concerns.

Foster carers highlighted good social work support and intervention as the single most important influence in successful problem solving. Link workers echoed this view, with most highlighting good team working as the most important factor for success:

> *If a child has a social worker who really believes in the foster carer and values their role, that is when things work best.* (Link worker)

The majority of foster carers were very complimentary about young people's social workers:

> *The social worker that we have at the moment . . . is fantastic. He cares greatly . . . I think any problems that I had with fostering have disappeared since this social worker's come on the scene.* (Foster carer)

> *The social workers for Janine were excellent. Absolutely excellent. They protected her. They protected us. They kept us fully informed . . . Her workers have been really, really brilliant.* (Foster carer)

However, foster carers saw poor social work intervention as the biggest hindrance to problem solving. They regarded poor support from link workers as having far less impact on the outcome of problem solving than poor support from social workers. Up to 20 per cent of the foster carers in our study felt support from young people's current social worker was less than adequate:

> *A lot of social workers treat you like glorified childminders.* (Foster carer)

> *Sometimes [social workers] cause the problems.* (Foster carer)

Link workers also highlighted poor social work intervention as the most significant hindrance to problem solving. But they were also conscious of failings in the fostering unit and foster carers' own limitations. Link workers again spoke of the clashes of personalities that sometimes made problems worse:

> *There had been problems between the [fostering] unit and the social worker . . . basically she didn't like the carers and I think that got in the way of the job.* (Link worker)

Link workers saw difficulties arise when the input from young people's social workers was minimal or where foster carers were undervalued by social workers. They also reported the negative effects of bureaucratic inefficiencies, refusal of requests for financial support and delays in providing services. These failures were seen as corrosive, gradually eating away at the goodwill of foster carers. Link workers sometimes felt powerless when constrained by budgets or the intransigence of management.

Line managers frequently dealt with issues raised by link workers and social workers. Fostering managers in particular reported feeling very accessible to foster carers:

> *Foster carers know that if they have a problem that needs a management decision, it's not that they're going behind their link worker's back . . . they just need some sort of response immediately.* (Fostering manager)

Senior social work managers were likely to get involved in problem solving only where issues or disagreements had become entrenched. Issues dealt with by senior managers frequently involved concerns about social work intervention or inaction. Managers shared the views of link workers that disagreements, particularly between foster carers and social workers, often had more to do with the personalities involved than practice and policy. But as one senior manager reflected:

> *We're in the human being business . . . I challenge anyone to come up with something that accounts for human beings and their differences.* (Senior social work manager)

The following two tables summarise the responses given by foster carers and link workers about what works well in problem solving for foster carers and what doesn't. They are a good illustration of the similarities and differences in perceptions.

Table 16: What works in problem solving for foster carers

| What works in problem solving | |
| --- | --- |
| **FOSTER CARERS** | **SOCIAL WORKERS** |
| • Good social work intervention and support, including:<br>– prompt practical help<br>– praise for foster carers<br>– listening<br>– good communication<br>– persistence with difficulties<br>– continuity<br>– availability and willingness to help<br>• Good support and intervention from link workers, including:<br>– availability and willingness to help<br>• Support from others<br>– other agencies<br>– birth family<br>– other carers<br>– senior mangers<br>• Foster carers' own resourcefulness | • Team approach, including:<br>– foster carer, social worker and link worker working together<br>– mutual support<br>– shared responsibility<br>– young person seen as priority<br>• Link worker intervention, including:<br>– availability and willingness to help<br>– listening and understanding<br>– promoting confidence<br>– liaison with social workers<br>– prompt practical help<br>• Foster carers' efforts, including:<br>– excellent communication/ listening skills<br>– excellent parenting skills<br>– commitment to young person |

Table 17: What doesn't work in problem solving for foster carers

| What doesn't work in problem solving | |
| --- | --- |
| **FOSTER CARERS** | **SOCIAL WORKERS** |
| • Poor social work intervention and support, including:<br> – indifference to difficulties<br> – not listening<br> – poor communication<br> – indecision<br> – poor decision making<br> – lack of financial support for young person<br> – inaction<br> – delays in action<br> – insensitivity/ unprofessional conduct<br> – ignoring young people<br> – social workers not available when needed<br> – ineffectiveness of emergency duty team<br>• Poor support from link workers, including:<br> – lack of financial support<br> – lack of practical help<br> – lack of emotional support during crisis<br>• Mistakes/ lack of experience of foster carers<br>• Lack of solution – tried everything, but still nothing works | • Poor social work intervention and support, including:<br> – lack of communication/ not listening/ ignored<br> – no support/ services in dealing with birth families/ school exclusions/ violent behaviour<br> – bureaucratic delays<br> – lack of financial support<br> – carers undervalued/ disliked by social workers<br> – lack of permanency planning<br> – alienation when allegation made<br>• Poor support from fostering unit, including:<br> – lack of support from link worker due to sickness/ leave/ staff vacancies<br> – delays in payments<br> – lack of respite provision<br> – lack of funding for storage/ transport especially for larger families<br>• Foster carers' limitations, including:<br> – carers feeling 'out of their depth'<br> – carers over-reacting<br> – carers not following advice<br> – carers stipulating very strict criteria about the young people they will foster |

# Discussion

Looking at the responses foster carers gave to the scenarios, it is clear that they take a great deal of personal responsibility in trying to resolve problems. Their comments reflect a high level of commitment and persistence on behalf of the young people in their care. The responses also demonstrate that carers employ different strategies to solve different problems. In some circumstances, carers initially take considerable responsibility, consulting people or asking for help only when their own efforts are unsuccessful. In other situations they rely substantially on help from social workers, again turning to link workers and managers if this help is not forthcoming.

The findings give us an overview of how influential foster carers perceive social workers and link workers to be in problem solving. Most foster carers (80 per cent or more) are complimentary about the input of both social workers and their link workers, but they see the interventions of social workers as far more influential on the outcomes of problem solving. Where help from social workers is prompt, consistent and well directed, problems are resolved well. But where this doesn't happen and foster carers feel poorly supported by social workers, solving problems is greatly hindered.

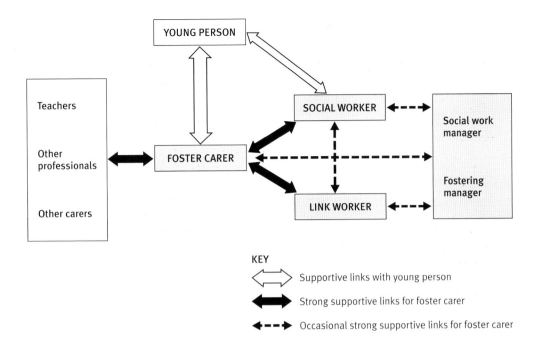

Diagram 5: Foster carers' problem solving network – as identified by foster carers

Link workers are generally seen as the 'backbone' of support for foster carers, available when needed to offer advice or chase up others. Yet only a small minority of foster carers mention poor support from link workers as hindering problem solving.

Looking at the problems that foster carers identify, the general strategies they describe are similar to the strategies they report for addressing young people's problems. The foster carers' problem solving network illustrated in Diagram 5, above, is very similar to the young people's problem solving network described by carers in the previous chapter (*see* Diagram 4, page 48). But for foster carers the extended network takes on more importance. There are stronger supportive links with link workers, managers and other professionals, demonstrating foster carers' capabilities in eliciting the help they need. Where supportive links with social workers and/ or link workers are poor (as described by about 20 per cent of foster carers) links to managers and others are of much greater importance. Foster carers stress the importance of knowing which workers to contact and who is most likely to help. This knowledge comes from experience, suggesting that inexperienced carers may not have the same confidence or skills in using this extended network effectively.

## Link workers

Link workers report that problem solving works best when all involved work together as a team. Problems are minimal where there is good communication and mutual support between the foster carer, link worker and the young person's social worker.

The views expressed by link workers are very similar to those described by foster carers. Link workers regard the majority of foster carers as well supported by both link workers and young people's social workers. How involved link workers become in problem solving depends on the problem concerned and how confident and skilled foster carers are. They report being involved to a greater extent if carers are inexperienced or where foster carers' own efforts have been unsuccessful.

Link workers express a general sense of 'parental' concern over the foster carers they support. Much of the intervention reported is aimed at reducing pressures on foster carers and trying to maintain channels of communication with all involved. Link workers saw the effectiveness of problem solving diminish where the input of young people's social workers was minimal, planning was poor or where carers felt undervalued. Their responses confirm the views of foster carers where specific problem solving is concerned. That is, the involvement of the young person's social worker has a more significant influence on the outcome of problem solving than the input of link workers.

In common with foster carers, link workers recognise the problem solving network illustrated in Diagram 5. Link workers, though, see an even more complex picture, involving further layers of management. Senior social services managers have a role to play where problems become particularly entrenched or where conflicts in personality hinder the resolution of problems.

## Conclusion

In this chapter we have identified strategies foster carers use in trying to resolve problems they identify. Carers rely on their own confidence and abilities to a high degree. Link workers provide the ongoing support for carers, but where specific problems are concerned carers look for effective intervention from young people's social workers. Where this is not forthcoming, foster carers readily enlist the help of link workers and line managers to resolve difficulties.

If we look back to the previous chapter we can see that foster carers use very similar strategies to address both problems that they themselves identify, and problems that young people might identify. The main differences are: the greater recognition of the role of the link worker; and that foster carers appear to enlist the help of the extended network more readily to help resolve problems that they themselves identify.

Foster carers and link workers share similar expectations for problem solving. They both recognise that where specific problem solving is concerned, it is the involvement of the young person's social worker (rather than the link worker) that has the greatest influence on outcome. If we look at the experience of social workers reported in Chapter 2 (page 18), many of the social workers interviewed had little experience of foster care and perhaps underestimate the importance of their role. There is a need for this role to be emphasised within social services departments to ensure foster carers receive the level of support they need.

# Summary

### Foster carers

- The strategies foster carers use to solve problems they experience vary depending on the type of problem.

- Where information on a young person is not readily available, foster carers report considerable reliance on social workers to resolve the problem. They may seek the assistance of their link worker and social worker's manager if necessary.

- Foster carers accept a high degree of responsibility in managing pressures to accept emergency placements, in order to minimise the disruption to other members of the household.

- Foster carers tend to regard cancelled meetings as an inevitable hazard of working with social services. If this is problematic they again accept responsibility for making sure their needs are taken into consideration.

- For issues such as making an optician's appointment for a young person, foster carers report taking full responsibility to resolve any difficulties.

- Where carers are concerned about the actions of a social worker or are trying to speed up a social work decision, foster carers show considerable determination and persistence in chasing the social workers and trying to rectify the situation for the young person. They expect to take the lead, but will involve managers and link workers as necessary.

- Where a young person experiences frequent changes of social worker, foster carers sometimes feel powerless as they have no control over changes of personnel. They are likely to rely on their link workers and social work managers to effect at least some control and minimise disruption for the young person.

- About 80 per cent of foster carers feel well supported by link workers and young people's social workers.

- Foster carers identify good social worker support and intervention as the key factor in successful problem solving.

- Foster carers identify poor social work intervention as the factor that most hinders successful problem solving.

- Foster carers use very similar strategies to address both problems that they themselves identify, and problems that young people might identify. The main differences are: the greater recognition of the role of the link worker; and that foster carers appear to enlist the help of the extended network more readily to help resolve problems that they themselves identify.

### Link workers

- Link workers vary their involvement in problem solving with foster carers depending on the problem concerned.

- Involvement varies depending on how confident or successful foster carers are at resolving problems themselves. Only where foster carers are unsuccessful do link workers expect to play a significant role – a view supported by foster carers.

- Link workers share the view that the majority of foster carers are well supported by both link workers and young people's social workers, but a minority (around 15 per cent) do not receive good support.

- Link workers recognise the importance of themselves, social workers, line managers and senior social services managers in helping to resolve problems for foster carers.

- Link workers identify good team working between the foster carer, the link worker and the social worker as the most important factor in successful problem solving.

- Link workers identify poor social work intervention and support as the factor most likely to hinder problem solving. But they also recognise that failings by the fostering unit and foster carers' own limitations also contribute.

- Link workers provide continuity and consistency of support for foster carers, but where specific problem solving is concerned they see the role of the social worker as more influential on outcome.

# 6

# PARTICIPATION AND INFLUENCE

*If I'm really honest . . . I don't know what young people in our fostering services think about or feel about the care they're getting.* (Senior social services manager)

## Introduction

The idea that the views of service users should influence service development is, in theory, fairly well established. Putting this idea into practice is more challenging, especially when it involves services to children and young people. The Government's Quality Protects Initiative, introduced in 1998 to reform services for looked after children, seeks to ensure improvements in the quality of care they receive. Key tasks in the Initiative require local authorities to 'ensure that appropriate mechanisms are in place to listen to the views of children and young people about the services provided to them'. The initiative puts the onus on social services managers to 'make sure you are consulting children and listening to their views . . . ' (Quality Protects Framework, Department of Health, 1998 quoted in Department of Health (2000)).

This chapter looks first at how young people in foster care get their views across to social services managers and how influential their views are in the management process. As we have seen from the previous chapters, foster carers play a very important role in listening to young people and in making sure problems get resolved. They see at first hand where the successes and shortfalls in the service lie. This chapter also considers how foster carers get their views heard and how influential these views are on the development of services in foster care.

## Young people

There was considerable variation between young people, foster cares and social services staff regarding how well informed they felt social services were about young people's views. Questions to young people in this study were phrased broadly, allowing them to define for themselves who they considered 'social services' to be. Invariably young people saw 'social services' as meaning their social worker. When we look at young people's support network (*see* Diagram 2, page 46) this is not surprising. Social workers are the only direct contact with the department that young people generally have.

Sixty per cent of young people in this study felt that on an individual level, views they expressed were listened to by their social workers:

> *I like my social worker because when she talks to me about something . . . she listens to what I have to say.* (Girl, 13)

> *If they think something and I think something . . . they would listen and I can say what are my reasons.* (Girl, 15)

Others were not so positive, with 40 per cent feeling unsure or unconvinced their views were listened to:

> *I can't really make them listen. I want them to listen but . . .* (Boy, 12)

When asked specifically if what they say makes a difference, again nearly 60 per cent of young people responded positively. But in dialogue when we explored with young people how their views influenced social services their responses were quite different. Here the largest group either gave no response or said they had no idea how their views affected things. While this might be expected of the younger children interviewed (8–12 years) we found no statistical difference between these and the teenage group (13–18 years). Only about 35 per cent of the young people we spoke to were positive about the way their views influenced decisions. All of these comments related to young people's own circumstances, such as asking for and getting increased contact with their families. None of the comments made acknowledged the possibility of having any wider influence on social services. Young people realised that their own views and opinions are not overriding and that it is adults who make decisions, as this young girl illustrates:

> *If like I want . . . more contact with my mum then they'll try and sort it out for me but most of the time it's what they think is the right thing to do.* (Girl, 10)

More specific questions were put to foster carers, and to social services staff. They were asked if they considered social services managers to be well informed about the views of young people in foster carer. The results for each sample group are shown in the table below. Though responding to different questions, young people's responses are included for broad comparison.

**Table 18: Perceptions about social services' knowledge of young people's views**

| Statement: *Social services are well informed about the views of young people in foster care* | Percentage response | | |
|---|---|---|---|
| | Agree | Unsure/ disagree | Total |
| Young people | 60% | 40% | 100% (n=61) |
| Foster carers | 55% | 45% | 100% (n=56) |
| Social workers | 33% | 67% | 100% (n=18) |
| Link workers | 17% | 83% | 100% (n=18) |
| Senior managers | 25% | 75% | 100% (n=16) |

Foster carers generally shared the views expressed by young people. Just over half were positive about how well listened to young people are, but when asked how influential young people's views were, over 75 per cent of carers were dubious or negative about young people's ability to influence:

> *They listen to children more now . . . but whether they take a lot of notice of children I don't know.* (Foster carer)

> *They're certainly listened to . . . but I don't know what effect they have.* (Foster carer)

Some foster carers expressed very strong negative views:

> *They don't have a cat in hell's chance!* (Foster carer)

> *Fostering services aren't run really for the benefit of children . . . They're run within the constraints of a budget.* (Foster carer)

The majority of social services staff had little faith that social services managers were well informed about young people's views and, as the table and comments below illustrate, little expectation that young people's views were influential.

**Table 19: Perceptions of foster carers and social services staff about young people's influence on social services**

| Statement: *Young people's views influence social services* | Percentage response | | |
|---|---|---|---|
| | Agree | Unsure/ disagree | Total |
| Foster carers | 24% | 76% | 100% (n=56) |
| Social workers | 13% | 87% | 100% (n=18) |
| Link workers | 22% | 78% | 100% (n=18) |
| Senior managers | 33% | 67% | 100% (n=16) |

The largest proportion of comments from social workers, link workers and social services managers described how little influence, if any, young people in foster care were seen to have. Two of those interviewed asked if the question was serious, such was their disbelief that young people's views would have any impact at all on social services:

> *I don't think young people have any influence whatsoever over the way fostering services are run. I don't know that they actually have an avenue into it.* (Social worker)

> *I don't think that children are made aware that they're important people in this process.* (Link worker)

> *If it was 'I'm at risk here', that would get a response within the day as all child protection referrals do. But if it was more . . . 'My care plan isn't being delivered',*

> *I suspect there's a decreasing response . . . If you then have a child who was complaining a lot I would suspect the response to them would diminish as well.* (Senior manager)

> *I don't think they have much influence at all . . . We haven't been consulting them in the right way. They're not an easily accessible group in the way that children in residential care are.* (Senior manager)

There were those, however, who were very positive about listening to young people and the influence they could have on the fostering service:

> *I feel as a team we're very proactive in terms of looking at children's issues in foster care . . . It's as much my responsibility as it is the social worker's.* (Link worker)

> *We now have a scheme for 'harder to place' children . . . their behaviour and their reactions to care have shown us that what we call mainstream [fostering] is not for them . . . so we've devised a new scheme that fits their needs. So really, in a very positive way they have affected the development of the services.* (Fostering manager)

The majority of responses demonstrate that considerable improvements are needed within local authorities if the Quality Protects Key Task to consult with young people (including those in foster care) are to be met. Each of the groups interviewed identified a variety of routes by which young people could make their views known. The next section explores the main routes in more detail, looking at both successes and limitations.

## Feedback routes

Different ways in which young people get their views heard were explored with each of the sample groups: i.e. young people, foster carers, social workers, link workers and social services managers. The main routes identified were via:

- social workers
- reviews
- foster carers.

### Social workers

This was the route most frequently recognised by young people, foster carers and social workers. Through developing good relationships with the young person, social workers are able to gather young people's views and pass these on to managers in regular supervision:

> *I suppose the social worker has a key role here. It's up to the social worker to pass on the children's views to their managers.* (Social worker)

Many of the young people's responses, though, reflected a high degree of supposition about how views were passed on rather than actual knowledge:

> *I tell the social worker and the social worker tells the boss, I think.* (Girl, 12)

Young people and foster carers recognised that social workers made choices about the information they passed on to managers. They saw difficult problems as more likely to be passed on rather than positive comments:

> *You tell your social worker and if it's bad then she'd tell them.* (Girl, 13)

> *The only time [young people] seem to input is if [it's] something negative . . . It's just sad that it has to be the bad things that get things rolling . . . where something's worked well, nothing's done about it.* (Foster carer)

> *I think if a young person is happy in a placement there can be a tendency to leave well alone. I think the only way that they would have any influence is if they really kicked off on a regular basis.* (Foster carer)

Social workers themselves had reservations about how effective they were at passing on young people's views to managers:

> *The majority of information goes through us, both for the carers and the children . . . and of course we have our own agendas . . . so their views are edited by us, if you like.* (Social worker)

> *In supervision [young people's views] could come up but I doubt it goes beyond principal level generally.* (Social worker)

> *If you're talking about managers who make changes in policies and procedures . . . it would have to be a really big thing before they'd be interested.* (Social worker)

For social workers to be an effective route for feeding back young people's views there has to be good relationships and good dialogue between them and the young people. We have seen that young people in the minority unsupported group (identified in Chapters 3 and 4) do not have such trusting relationships with their social workers. For this group in particular, social workers are unlikely to be an effective feedback route:

> *I don't tell social services nothing . . . They're not even bothered.* (Girl, 16)

Even those who said they would confide in their social workers were sometimes disillusioned by their response:

> *I asked for a police check and stuff, they never listened . . . same as I've asked to see my grandma but they haven't looked into it much.* (Boy, 12)

> *Some social workers I've had in the past don't understand what you're talking about.* (Boy, 12)

A small number of young people were very positive about their own involvement and influence in planning and making decisions. They were very complimentary about the role of their social workers:

> *I say a lot anyway. They helped me a lot giving me a social worker.* (Girl, 10)

Though social workers are perhaps the most obvious route by which young people's views can be passed on to managers, it is clear from the comments above that many limitations exist.

### Reviews

Statutory childcare reviews, held every six months for looked after children, provide another mechanism for feeding back young people's views to managers. There is an expectation that most young people will participate in their reviews in some way – through attending meetings, completing forms or passing on their views through another person (foster carers, social worker, parent, etc.). Bond and Pickerden (2000), though, noted that the ability of children to express opinions during a review process often rested on the quality of the relationship between the child and the social worker. Again, for the young people in the minority unsupported group who do not have good relationships with their social workers, reviews are unlikely to offer an alternative for their voices to be heard.

Comments about how effective reviews are in getting young people's views across varied in this study. Some were positive about the process:

> *Well, when you have a review you tell people and they pass it on to their bosses.* (Girl, 16)

> *Duncan is using his reviews much more effectively now. At his last one he didn't put much on his form, but this time round he had a lot more to say. That's worked well.* (Social worker)

Others expressed reservation:

> *They come and sit in your reviews don't they? There's always one high up person that comes . . . she sits there thinking that she knows what I want . . . They just twist things.* (Girl, 16)

> *The review forms, they can have their little say of their own . . . And then there's these action plans, when they write down a lot of things about how they feel . . . But they're a bit over the kids' heads really.* (Foster carer)

> *Before 1992, I think all copies of reviews went to the area manager . . . and were looked at . . . but I don't think they go anywhere. I don't think generally it's passed up to senior managers.* (Link worker)

Each of the local authorities taking part in this study had recently introduced an independent reviewing process. The reviewing teams manage and chair statutory childcare reviews independent of social work line management. The perception of reviewing officers and senior managers interviewed was that young people's views were listened to in relation to day-to-day care, but there was no collation of those views for management purposes. Where a reviewing officer might pass on information, it was usually to a specific manager about a specific child. Reviewing officers expressed the aspiration that the review process could produce more collated information in the future, but the volume of current work meant this was not a priority:

> *I think generally young people's views come through . . . But we don't get any kind of broad picture . . . I would hope that as the reviewing team develops that's the sort of thing we will be able to get.* (Reviewing officer)

> *What you get from reviewing officers is individual problems . . . but no systematic approach really.* (Senior manager)

> *We've got to look at making the system of feedback through review better . . . more child friendly . . . finding better ways of eliciting the views of foster children . . . I could say, if I'm really honest, that I don't know what young people in our fostering services think about or feel about the care they're getting.* (Senior manager)

Clearly, statutory childcare reviews offer a valuable framework for collating young people's views, but it would appear local authorities are missing these opportunities. How well young people participate in their reviews depends on a number of factors: how willing young people are to engage; the help, encouragement and preparation young people receive before reviews; and how receptive adults are to listening to young people. Hogan and Sinclair (1997) commented that many young people in care found attending reviews either a boring irrelevance or a frustrating and disempowering experience. Interestingly, Bond and Pickerden (2000) found that foster carers, despite being the people who carry out the day-to-day care of young people, had little involvement in preparing young people for reviews, a perception shared by the foster carers we spoke to in this study.

### Foster carers

Although adults recognised foster carers as a potential route through which young people could feed back their views to service managers, very few young people saw this as their carers' role. Where young people did mention their carers it was as facilitators, passing on information to social workers:

> *If you tell [foster carers] they can . . . phone the social worker up to let them know.* (Girl, 10)

Most foster carers tended to agree with this view, seeing themselves as a link in the chain. But some carers saw their role as much more proactive, acting as advocates for young people in their care and ensuring young people's comments were directed to the right people.

> *It's my job as well. I mean, I'm there to fight for that child for whatever that child needs. I'd advocate for a child.* (Foster carer)

Foster carers also reported taking on greater responsibility if the social worker was unavailable. This role was recognised by managers:

> *If there was no social worker . . . for whatever reason, foster carers would be*

*advocating certain things on that child's behalf. That would come directly from the foster carer to us.* (Senior manager)

How important the foster carer is in feeding back young people's views to social services managers depends on the division of responsibilities between the foster carer and the social worker and, importantly, who a young person chooses to confide in. As we have seen earlier (*see* Chapter 3), for the majority of young people in foster care, the person they are most likely to confide in is their foster carer. Reasons why foster carers are not seen to have a more prominent role in feeding back young people's views were put forward by one fostering manager. This manager saw many of the day-to-day issues raised by young people absorbed by foster carers into the daily round of family life. Although a young person may be trying to raise an issue, it was likely to be seen as just part of the daily grumbles of living together. Unless the issue came to the attention of the social worker it would remain within the household. Even if the social worker was aware and discussed the issue with the young person and the carer, it would have to be something exceptional to find its way out of the core triangle (i.e. young person, foster carer, social worker). The consequence of this is that young people's views are not fed back to managers – a view acknowledged by this foster carer:

*I think there's a lot of young children out there with a lot of knowledge and a lot to say but sometimes it just gets lost.* (Foster carer)

## Improving young people's participation

We asked all the groups within this study how young people could have more say and more influence on social services. Young people were particularly unsure, and their responses are summarised in the table below.

Table 20: Young people's views on how to have more say within social services

| Ideas on how to have more say | Percentage response (n=61) |
|---|---|
| No response/ don't know/ not interested/ influence impossible | 58% |
| More contact with social worker and support at meetings | 20% |
| Have enough say already | 13% |
| Other: group activities/ surveys/ booklets | 9% |
| Total | 100% |

The majority gave no response or could not think of ways they could influence social services. The most frequent constructive comments were about the role of social workers. Young people wanted more frequent contact and better support in meetings, feeling this would give them more say in the process. Some told us how difficult it was for them to speak up and make their views known:

*You have to be brave and shout at them.* (Boy, 11)

Others described how undervalued they felt when social workers didn't keep to their commitments:

> *They don't come and see me enough . . . They're meant to come every six weeks but they don't. They come when they're ready to come . . . It makes you feel like you've done something wrong to them . . . because they don't want to come and see me.* (Girl, 16)

Over one-third of foster carers gave no response or did not know how to improve young people's influence. The majority, however, felt the onus was on social services and, in particular, social workers, to make time for young people. The most frequent constructive comment foster carers made was, again, that social workers should spend more time with children and families:

> *I think social workers need to spend more time with children. I don't think there's actually an awful lot of sitting down and talking to them.* (Foster carer)

Foster carers' responses are summarised in the table below.

**Table 21: Foster carers' views on how to improve young people's influence within social services**

| Ways young people can have greater influence | Percentage response (n=56) |
|---|---|
| No response/ don't know | 35% |
| Social worker spending more time with children and families | 28% |
| Group activities for foster families/ workshops/ conferences | 15% |
| Managers to listen to young people and act on what is said | 10% |
| Foster carers being more open, encouraging and loving | 5% |
| Other | 7% |
| Total | 100% |

Social workers, link workers and social services managers were ambivalent about how best to improve the influence of young people in foster care, but the role of the social worker was again emphasised:

> *It would be massively improved if the social workers had more time to spend with the young people and with the foster carers.* (Social worker)

But as we have seen above, there were also doubts about how effective social workers really are in passing on young people's views:

> *In foster homes it's so difficult because you're working within a family unit and behind closed doors. You really don't know what goes on in any family.* (Social worker)

> *I've had lots of foster children . . . in permanent placements and I don't want to be part of their lives . . . It's not normal to have someone coming in from outside, so I feel uncomfortable about that.* (Social worker)

There was also ambivalence about the merits or likely success of group activities such as support groups or conference-type events. Group activities were seen to emphasise the fact that the young people were different and were therefore unlikely to attract much interest. Others had experience of very successful events involving young people in foster care. Social services staff talked about the need for creativity and imagination to make consultation with young people in foster care effective:

> *I think we've been too driven by the residential model. We need to be moving away from that. Stop thinking you can use the same techniques in foster care.* (Senior manager)

Themes emphasised more by managers included using existing systems, such as reviews, more creatively and pulling together the information already available:

> *I suppose you could try and set up a group for young people . . . but the whole point of foster care is you're trying to normalise their lives. Possibly the only way of doing this is to collate information from reviews, the information from social workers or do research where you actually sample groups of children from foster care . . . You can get quite a lot on an individual basis but it's pulling it together that's difficult.* (Senior manager)

## Foster carers

We can see that mechanisms for feeding back young people's views are not well developed, but as the primary carers for young people, foster carers are in a unique position to provide reflections on how well services are delivered. We have seen that with young people's views, foster carers act as a link in the chain, passing on information and viewpoints to social workers and statutory reviews. If we return to Chapter 5 we see the effort and determination foster carers put into resolving the various problems they encounter. If intervention from young people's social workers is not forthcoming, they readily enlist the help of link workers and line managers to resolve difficulties. What is not so clear is how well foster carers' views are fed back up the hierarchical chain to the senior managers and policy makers.

We asked foster carers and social services staff how well informed they felt social services are about the views of foster carers. A small majority of foster carers (58 per cent) and managers (56 per cent) were confident that foster carers' views were listened to. But most social workers and link workers, and a sizeable minority of carers and managers, were not so sure. These perceptions are summarised in Table 22 opposite.

If we compare these results to those in Table 18 on page 74 we see managers feel much better informed about foster carers' views than about the views of young people. The majority of managers (nearly 70 per cent) were also optimistic about the influence foster carers have. But this was not a view shared by most foster carers, link workers or social workers, as Table 23 and comments opposite illustrate.

Table 22: Perceptions of foster carers and social services staff on how well informed social services are of foster carers' views

| Statement:<br>*Social services are well informed about the views of foster carers* | Percentage response | | |
|---|---|---|---|
| | Agree | Unsure/ disagree | Total |
| Foster carers | 58% | 42% | 100% (n=56) |
| Social workers. | 17% | 83% | 100% (n=18) |
| Link workers | 28% | 72% | 100% (n=18) |
| Managers | 56% | 44% | 100% (n=16) |

Table 23: Perceptions of foster carers and social services staff on foster carers' influence on social services

| Statement:<br>*Foster carers' views influence social services* | Percentage response | | |
|---|---|---|---|
| | Agree | Unsure/ disagree | Total |
| Foster carers | 34% | 66% | 100% (n=18) |
| Social workers | 6% | 94% | 100% (n=18) |
| Link workers | 33% | 67% | 100% (n=18) |
| Social services managers | 69% | 31% | 100% (n=16) |

*I've discussed specific issues that have made people think again, but in terms of general fostering . . . I don't think really I have a lot of influence there.* (Foster carer)

*When you think about what an incredible job foster carers are doing . . . they don't have a very high status in the department. I feel very often that foster carers are viewed not as partners but as clients almost.* (Link worker)

*I feel the service tends to be more influenced by resources or the lack of resources, by the lack of choice for children . . . Those things are much more influential than the views of carers.* (Manager)

Where managers spoke optimistically about foster carers' influence, they were positive about the roles of foster care associations or liaison groups. Foster carers and social services staff each identified a variety of routes by which foster carers could make their views known. The next section explores the main routes briefly, looking at both successes and limitations.

## Feedback routes

While the feedback routes for young people were seen to be limited, those identified for foster carers were more varied. Those most frequently mentioned were:

- via link workers
- direct contact with line managers and occasionally senior managers (e.g. meetings, letters, telephone calls)
- via young people's social workers

- childcare reviews
- foster carers' annual reviews
- local or national foster care associations/ liaison groups
- foster carer support groups.

In addition to these avenues, smaller numbers of foster carers and managers also mentioned various workshops, consultation meetings and training events. Some managers and link workers mentioned assessment forms completed by foster carers at the end of a placement. Two managers and one social worker also mentioned the complaints procedure as a way for foster carers to feed back their viewpoints.

### Link worker

Link workers were seen by carers and social services staff as being the main route for the feedback of foster carers' views. Most of the carers we interviewed felt they had very good relationships with their link workers:

> *I find I get on very well with my link worker and if I have any views to express I can tell her.* (Foster carers)

> *I always tell our link worker . . . He goes to the head of service or the one above.* (Foster carer)

But not all carers were so optimistic that their views are passed up the hierarchical structure:

> *Whether [my views] are acted upon . . . is a different matter.* (Foster carer)

The majority (78 per cent) of link workers saw themselves as the primary vehicle for representing foster carers' views. They described discussing issues that carers raised within the fostering team and, where appropriate, these were passed on by the team leaders to higher management:

> *The service managers meet monthly . . . [the unit manager] will quite often go to that and report.* (Link worker)

> *If there was enough of us in a team meeting who had similar things coming from carers there's the possibility that we could take it to a management meeting.* (Link worker)

Yet, we see in Tables 22 and 23 that most link workers have severe doubts that senior managers are well informed or influenced by foster carers' views. Most of the information passed on by link workers was not collated for management. Those issues that were passed on tended to focus on specific difficulties, e.g. liaison with social workers, payment structures and school exclusions. Many link workers were frustrated by the lack of attention paid to foster carers' views, expressing concern about their low status both locally and nationally:

> *It's wrapped up in the argument about whether carers are volunteers or part of a professional team . . . and that's a national issue.* (Link worker)

*They should be listened to because at the end of the day our fostering service depends on them and without the carers there's no service.* (Link worker)

### Direct communication with managers

We have seen in previous chapters that when problems are not being resolved, foster carers are generally confident about communicating directly with line managers, and both foster carers and managers saw this direct communication as a valuable tool for views to be expressed:

> *If I had any views that I thought were really important I'd just go straight to the manager anyway.* (Foster carer)

But there were again doubts about how far up the management structure carers' views would travel:

> *I know it can go up to the team manager, but I don't really know how far it gets.* (Foster carer)

Senior fostering managers reported receiving telephone calls and letters direct from foster carers, and a dedicated answer service for foster carers in one authority was seen as a very effective direct route to senior management. But, again, matters raised in this way tended to be about individual circumstances rather than broader issues. Interestingly, this direct communication was rarely mentioned by link workers as a possible avenue for carers to express their views.

### Social workers

Social workers received a great deal of information from foster carers, especially about their views on the individual young people in their care. As with young people's views, these were likely to be discussed in supervision meetings with their line managers:

> *If a foster carer raised a concern then it would probably be talked about in supervision.* (Social worker)

> *In my experience foster carers pass their views to social workers very readily.* (Social worker)

Yet again there were doubts expressed by both social workers and foster carers about how far up the management structure carers' views are passed on:

> *Sometimes you can pass on information to social workers but it tends to be put . . . to the bottom of the pile.* (Foster carer)

We can see from Table 23 that social workers had severe doubts about the influence foster carers' views have. Social workers generally saw themselves as too distant from fostering practice to be able to comment. This raises the question as to what social workers do with the information given to them by foster carers. Managers were conscious that this information was often lost:

> *[Foster carers] will sort it out [with] . . . the social worker usually, and that's as far as it generally goes.* (Senior manager)

### Childcare reviews

Each of the groups interviewed acknowledged childcare reviews as a possible avenue for foster carers to express views, but these were generally limited to views about specific young people. Social workers particularly commented that:

> *Carers . . . can be very vocal at child care reviews.* (Social worker)

But, as we have seen earlier, information from statutory childcare reviews is not collated in any coherent form for management purposes.

### Foster carers' reviews

Interestingly, very few foster carers recognised their own yearly reviews as an opportunity to share their views with the department. This was more often highlighted as a possible route by social services staff.

### Foster care associations/liaison groups

Senior managers regarded local foster care associations to be an important focus for dialogue with foster carers. However, the importance given to these varied between the local authorities studied. In one authority the group met regularly with the senior management team including the director. Foster carers with links to this group regarded meetings as very effective:

> *We've got an agreement with [the department] that before they put anything in writing to say it's going to happen, we get notification first and we discuss it . . . The director decides he'll back off on certain things sometimes.*
> (Foster carer)

But only a small percentage of foster carers saw organised associations as an effective route to get their views heard. Most felt such groups were unrepresentative of the majority of carers, a view shared by some link workers and line mangers:

> *There are very few people who attend the local organisation so it's a very sort of set group.* (Link worker)

There is clearly a discrepancy here between the views of senior managers and those of front-line workers and most foster carers.

### Other routes

In one of the local authorities studied, local support groups were seen as another possible route for foster carers to make their views known. But in the other two authorities these groups were seen more as opportunities for mutual support, rather than as an instrument to feed back views to managers.

Foster carers mentioned the occasional large meetings called by the department to gauge foster carers' views. These were either specific events as part of, for example, a departmental inspection process, or more regular training workshops. Some senior managers were positive about the information they gained from these and were confident that issues raised informed service planning.

### Improving foster carers' participation

Generally foster carers saw any influence they had as localised. When asked about how foster carers could have more influence on the fostering service, carers tended to answer in terms of their work with individual young people rather than looking at their involvement more strategically. Many commented on the lack of true partnership with social services. As the people who cared for the young people 24 hours a day, foster carers felt they were in a very good position to understand young people's needs and feelings. Yet carers often described having their views dismissed by social workers and ignored at childcare reviews. The improvement foster carers called for most frequently was to have their views listened to and respected more by social workers.

Foster carers regarded senior managers as being too far removed from carers' daily experience, and failing to understand their reality. Some carers in our study felt they could be more involved in fostering in general and suggested a number of ways this could be achieved, including:

- regular meetings, training events, support groups attended by senior managers
- involvement in social work training
- better promotion of the role of local fostering associations
- membership of the National Foster Care Association.

Others felt their lives were too busy looking after the young people to be able to contribute on a strategic level, commenting that they were already snowed under with paperwork and did not need any more.

Link workers supported the suggestions made by foster carers above. They saw scope for carers to be much more involved in the training of staff and other foster carers, and supported the promotion of carers' support groups, regular meetings with senior managers and regular consultations. Managers again suggested initiatives such as training, planning educational provision for looked after children and more regular consultation. There was a desire expressed by managers to see foster carers more involved as partners in the system:

> *I think there are far more ways we could use foster carers' perspectives in terms of corporate parenting . . . if you want to raise the outcomes for young people you've got to empower the carers more because they're the ones that will really be the advocates for that child.* (Senior manager)

## Discussion

### Young people

If we look at the main routes available for young people to feed back their views, we see there is a strong tendency for their views to remain within the core triangle of support identified in earlier chapters (i.e. between the young person, foster carer and social worker – *see* Diagram 6 overleaf). Where information is shared outside this triangle, it is likely to be dealt with on an individual basis rather than collectively.

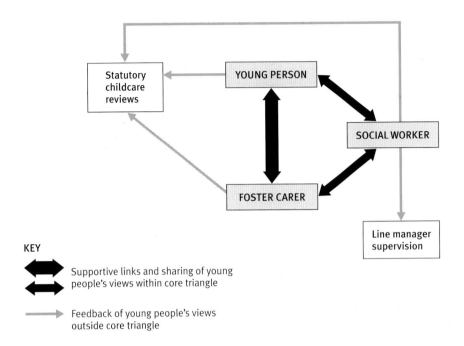

**KEY**

➤➤ Supportive links and sharing of young people's views within core triangle

→ Feedback of young people's views outside core triangle

**Diagram 6: Feedback of young people's views within and outside young people's support network – as identified by majority well-supported group**

Feedback, via social workers or foster carers, to line managers and reviews effectively reaches a dead-end. Comments from those interviewed in this study highlight the fact that information is not collated or passed on in any structured form. This means there are very limited possibilities for young people in foster care to have influence at a managerial level. Where young people reported their voices as having a positive impact, this centred on their own individual circumstances rather than the possibility of having any wider influence.

For the young people in the majority well-supported group, with a network of strong supportive links, their views are likely to be shared freely within the core triangle. There is likely to be a significant amount of information available, but this is rarely passed on to managers. This information is neither accessed nor utilised by policy makers. There is clearly a great deal of potential for local authorities to make use of this shared information and incorporate this, in a structured way, into the planning and development of services.

For the minority unsupported group of young people, where supportive links within the core triangle are weak, sharing of views is likely to be very limited or perhaps not well received. It follows that information flowing outside this triangle will be minimal and most likely focused on the negative aspects of a young person's behaviour (*see* Diagram 7 opposite). For this group of young people, the fact that their views are not easily shared, even with those who care for them, hinders the ability of local authorities to understand or plan alternative structures to meet their needs.

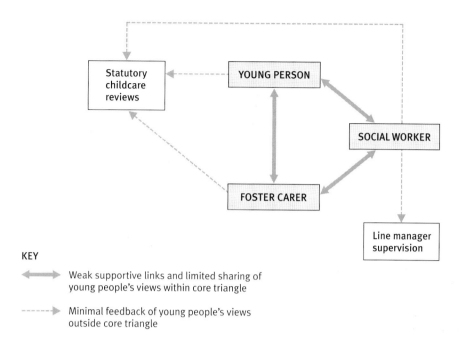

KEY

⟷ Weak supportive links and limited sharing of
young people's views within core triangle

- - - ▶ Minimal feedback of young people's views
outside core triangle

**Diagram 7: Feedback of young people's views within and outside young people's support network – as identified by minority unsupported group**

Where managers do acknowledge young people's influence on services, they describe the local authority reacting to young people's behaviour rather than responding to consultation or comment. Considerable improvements are needed if local authorities are serious about meeting Quality Protects Key Tasks to consult with young people. Finding ways to access the information available within the young person's core triangle of support must be a priority. Authorities need to look at imaginative and creative ways of using the reviewing process, strengthen the role of the social worker and pay greater attention to the wealth of knowledge gathered by foster carers. Managers also need to be more accessible to young people and should take the lead in ensuring young people's views are collated and used to influence planning.

## Foster carers

The variety of routes by which foster carers can potentially make their views known to social services managers contrasts with the limited routes identified by young people. Yet, as we have seen above, these avenues are not always effective or influential.

Managers in each local authority recognised the importance of contact with carers and expressed a commitment to listening to their views and a willingness to see carers as more involved partners. Some were particularly positive about the influence foster carers have, especially where group consultations had taken place or local foster care associations were active. Where foster carers were positive about the influence they could have on social services, they also saw this influence lying predominantly with organised foster care associations. However, as we have seen, there are questions about how representative such associations are.

There was a disparity between the views of managers and staff further down the line. Link workers and social workers felt views gleaned from foster carers generally focused on immediate issues affecting themselves or the young people they cared for – a view shared by foster carers. There were doubts expressed about how far up the management structure views were passed on and disappointment that there was so little collation of information to inform policy and practice.

Foster carers reported feeling dismissed by social workers and felt the most effective way of improving their influence within the service was for young people's social workers to listen to them more and to respect their views. If managers wish to see foster carers as more involved partners, relationships at this ground level need to change.

## Conclusion

What is clear from those we interviewed for this study is that potential avenues exist for both the views of young people and foster carers to be fed back to services managers. But these avenues are not being used effectively. Managers we spoke to expressed a commitment and willingness to see that young people and foster carers have greater influence on services, yet it is clear that the mechanisms to make this happen are poorly developed. A great deal of information is shared at the bottom of the chain, between young people, foster carers, social workers and link workers. Ways of collating this information systematically and ensuring this information is fed into the management process would greatly improve the influence carers and young people have on social services.

The comments of young people and foster carers show that social workers have a major role to play in passing on views and opinions. They play a key role in absorbing information from both young people and foster carers, yet much of this is lost. Line managers and senior managers need to look at how this wealth of information can be collated and used to inform service provision. While one-off consultations may be effective, social services departments need to establish a more systematic approach to gathering the views of carers and young people, ensuring this is integrated into the planning process.

## Summary

### Young people

- Most young people (60 per cent) and a small majority of foster carers (55 per cent) believe social services managers are well informed about young people's views. But this is not a view shared by the majority of social services staff (between 67 per cent and 83 per cent), and a sizeable minority of young people and foster carers (40 per cent and 45 per cent respectively).

- Social workers, foster carers and statutory childcare reviews are seen as the main routes by which young people's views may be fed back to social services managers.

- Where young people are positive about their involvement in planning and decision making, this focuses on their own individual circumstances rather than the possibility of having wider influence.

- Young people, foster carers and social services staff acknowledge that the amount of information passed on to management is limited. The perception is that only difficult problems or exceptional situations are likely to be passed on higher up the management line. The majority of foster carers and social services staff feel young people in foster care have very little influence on social services.

- Although information about individual young people is fed back to managers in staff supervision and statutory childcare reviews, this information effectively reaches a dead-end as it is not collated in any coherent form. Consequently there is no overview of young people's views from foster care and no accessible data for policy makers.

## Foster carers

- A small majority of foster carers (58 per cent) and managers (56 per cent) believe senior managers are well informed about the views of foster carers. But this is not a view shared by social workers, link workers and a sizeable minority of carers and managers.

- While managers are quite positive about the influence foster carers have on services, most foster carers, social workers and link workers feel foster carers have very little influence.

- Compared with the limited routes for young people, a variety of potential avenues were identified for feeding back the views of foster carers, including: via link workers, social workers, direct contact between carers and managers, childcare reviews, foster carers' annual reviews, foster care associations and one-off consultations.

- Managers are the most positive group about the influence of foster care associations and one-off consultations.

- Information about foster carers' individual situations is shared with social workers and link workers, but rarely collated for management purposes. There are doubts about how far up the management structure foster carers' views are passed on.

- Foster carers feel the most effective way to improve the influence they have on services is for young people's social workers to listen to them more and respect their views.

- Other ways of improving foster carers' influence on fostering services include: regular meetings, consultations, training events and support groups attended by senior managers; involvement in social work and foster carer training; and better promotion of the role of local fostering associations.

### Young people and foster carers

■ Potential avenues clearly exist for the views of both young people and foster carers to be fed back to social services managers. But these avenues are not being used effectively. Mechanisms to ensure young people's and foster carers' viewpoints influence service developments are poorly developed.

■ There is little evidence that local authorities are fulfilling their Quality Protects obligations to consult and listen to the views of young people or their foster carers, in any structured or continuous manner.

# 7

# THE COMPLAINTS PROCEDURE

*A lot of children don't know about the procedure. It's all right us adults knowing, but it's the children that have the complaints. They're the ones that need the information.* (Foster carer)

## Introduction

The introduction of the Representations and Complaints Procedure, in The Children Act 1989, sought to provide young people, particularly those in local authority care, with a formal procedure to address any complaints they had about the care they received. The procedure was developed out of a general move to make health and social services more accountable to service users, and followed a series of inquiries into the abuse of young people in care (Wallis and Frost, 1998). The procedure also specifically lists 'any local authority foster parent' among the limited number of people who may make a complaint about services to a child or young person, provided by a local authority (Department of Health, 1991).

With young people in foster care accounting for two out of every three looked after children, they are the largest potential users of the complaints procedure. But previous studies (e.g. Fletcher, 1993; Wallis and Frost, 1998) show young people in foster care have little knowledge and make little use of the procedure. When The Children Act was first implemented there was also optimism that the procedure would provide foster carers with an avenue to air grievances in an effective way. But this has also not been borne out in practice.

In this chapter we explore briefly the knowledge young people and foster carers have of the complaints procedure, and look at their reluctance to use the procedure to help resolve problems.

## Knowledge of the complaints procedure

### Young people

Of the 61 young people interviewed in this study, over half (55 per cent) had no knowledge at all about the complaints procedure. Only 35 per cent of young people had some knowledge, remembering conversations with social workers or leaflets and letters they had received. The remaining ten per cent knew they could complain to their social worker or foster carer but were not necessarily aware of any formal process, or the existence of a social services complaints officer. We found teenagers to be no better informed than younger children, but there were significant variations in knowledge depending on where young people lived. Knowledge of the procedure ranged from only 24 per cent in one local authority to 70 per cent in another. The difference reflected the way in which the complaints procedure was advertised in each local authority and the varying profiles of their respective complaints officers. In the local authority with the highest level of awareness, young people remembered receiving a letter about the procedure with the complaints officer's photograph on it. This was clearly a successful tactic that conveyed a message:

> *[The complaints officer] sends . . . letters to us every now and again with her picture at the bottom of the letter . . . She just says if there's any complaints either ring her or write to her.* (Girl, 10)

Only five young people in our study mentioned their social workers as a source of information, and when we spoke to social workers only a small minority expressed any confidence that the young people they worked with knew anything about the complaints procedure. The majority (83 per cent), across all three local authorities, were uncertain about how much young people knew, presuming it to be extremely little. Social workers were more likely to discuss problems with young people on a one-to-one basis and might mention the complaints procedure only as a last resort:

> *I always spend time alone with him then he can talk to me about it and we'll try to do something but I've never mentioned to him that in the local authority we have a complaints procedure.* (Social worker)

Social workers identified a number of blocks to young people acquiring knowledge about the complaints procedure:

- written material presuming an ability to read and understand information
- information provided in residential homes not sent to foster placements
- a young person's cognitive development
- new social workers presuming prior knowledge when taking over work with a young person
- lack of regular mailings, ignoring the temporary nature of most foster placements
- decisions made by social workers about when information is given
- lack of attention given to complaints at reviews.

### Foster carers

In contrast to the young people, the majority of foster carers (68 per cent) said they were aware of the complaints procedure, but this response encompassed their wide range of knowledge. Levels of awareness were similar across the three local authorities studied. Some had personal experience of using the complaints procedure and understood the process well. Others were aware of the existence of the procedure, or of the complaints officer, but knew very little detail:

> *I know I can complain. I'd probably do it through my [link] worker.*
> (Foster carer)

This still leaves nearly one-third of foster carers claiming to have little or no knowledge about their statutory right to raise complaints. Foster carers who did have some awareness, gained their knowledge mostly through leaflets, foster carers' handbooks/ fact files and through training. Yet link workers regarded themselves as one of the main providers of this information. However, some link workers recognised their own limitations in passing on information:

> *To be very frank, I'm not that au fait with the complaints procedure myself . . .*
> *It's not something I've come across. It's just something I read in the manual when*
> *I first started.* (Link worker)

> *They're [foster carers] probably aware of the complaints procedure, the fact that*
> *it exists and that they can make complaints, but probably not how to go about*
> *it – how the complaints procedure works.* (Link worker)

## Use of the complaints procedure

### Young people

Although only two of the young people in our study had any experience of contacting a complaints officer about problems, we explored situations in which each young person might make a complaint. Nearly 40 per cent of young people gave no response at all to such questions, but those who did most frequently mentioned the possibility of abuse or mistreatment as a reason to complain, followed by poor social work practice (such as where social workers failed to keep promises or ignored young people). In Chapter 4, young people identified being ignored by social workers as a major factor in diminishing their expectations of support in problem solving. For the minority group of young people who experience such poor support, the complaints procedure potentially offers a useful alternative in seeking help. But, as we have seen earlier, because most young people in foster care lack knowledge of the procedure, it is unlikely to be a real alternative in practice.

Most of the responses young people gave about potential uses of the complaints procedure were hypothetical. However, eight young people talked about real situations where they thought they could have made a complaint. Most involved poor social work practice rather than issues of abuse or mistreatment. Seven of the 56 foster carers we spoke to in this study reported helping a young person they had cared for make a complaint of some kind (not necessarily formal). Again, most were about poor social work practice (e.g. repeatedly cancelling visits or not turning up).

One of the few foster carers who had used the formal complaints procedure expressed frustration and dismay at the response they had received:

> *I went through the procedure of complaining about this social worker . . . His principal was making excuses for him . . . He forgets things and then if things go wrong it's like he's trying to blame everything on me and his standard of work and practice is beyond a joke . . . They're all going to stick with him on his little team . . . I'm just the carer . . . it [was] a waste of time.* (Foster carer)

Young people put the lack of use of the complaints procedure in foster care (compared with residential care) down to the differences in culture and environment. Few had experienced residential care, but most had very strong negative views about children's homes and presumed there was far greater justification for making complaints in a residential home. Perceptions included:

* an atmosphere of violence/ bad language/ drug taking in residential homes
* too many young people for staff to listen to/ no personal care
* staff don't have time for you/ don't love you/ don't really care
* staff change frequently/ get stressed out

In contrast, young people saw the positive aspects of living with a foster family and highlighted the lack of need to complain. Reasons given included:

* foster families are like a real family/ treat you like their own family
* foster carers care about you/ give you time and attention/ talk to you/ listen to you
* you get well looked after/ treated better than by your real mum
* foster carers can sort problems out for you.

The difference in perceptions are well illustrated by the following comments from young people:

> *People [in children's homes] have drugs and all that stuff and the adults are dead stressed so they hit you.* (Boy, 13)

> *Because foster families, you're like a household and . . . when you settle in it's like it's your own family . . . they treat you like you're their family.* (Boy, 12)

However, some young people spoke about the fear of the consequences of making a complaint in foster care or their lack of confidence to voice concerns. Fears focused on the assumption that making a complaint would inevitably cause conflict with their foster families and they might get moved to a children's home. Given the negative perceptions young people had about residential care, this was a very real fear.

Foster carers gave very similar responses to young people, stressing the differences between residential and foster care. They also saw the disparity of information given to young people in different settings. Their perception that young people in residential care are much better informed is supported by other authors, for example,

Fletcher (1993), Wallis and Frost (1998) and Utting (1997). Other comments focused on the lack of opportunity to complain in foster care, an unwillingness to approach social workers or not realising something was wrong:

> *Our long-term children didn't think of their social worker as being for them. They classed their social worker with us . . . as someone in authority over them.* (Foster carer)

> *They might not know it's wrong for the foster carer to . . . give them a clout across the back of the head. They might just think that, well, they got it at home so what's the difference.* (Foster carer)

Most social workers we spoke to had experience of supporting young people in residential care in making complaints, but all confirmed that the use of the procedure in foster care was extremely rare. Social workers tended to see the complaints procedure as adversarial and unhelpful in problem solving. It was seen as more of a blame exercise when things had gone wrong, or as a weapon young people might use against foster carers. They again spoke generally about the differences in culture and environment between residential and foster care, but some were candid about their reluctance to promote the complaints procedure in foster care, stressing the lack of alternative placements for young people should a complaint lead to a breakdown of relationships. Managers and reviewing officers agreed there was a tendency to look unfavourably at the use of the complaints procedure:

> *We would like to say that we always pick it up in reviews, but we don't . . . We only tend to remember about it when they're unhappy in their placement. Then we say, 'Did you know there's a complaints procedure?' and everybody else looks daggers at you from around the table as if to say, 'What are you telling them that for?'* (Reviewing officer)

Over a decade later, the original aspirations of The Children Act – that the complaints procedure would provide an avenue for young people to raise concerns formally – have clearly not been met. If we look at problem solving in terms of a continuum, the use of the complaints procedure by young people in foster care is likely to occur only at the far end of the line, if ever. The success of other problem solving methods (as described in Chapter 4), lack of knowledge or opportunity to complain, fear and lack of confidence all contribute to this.

## Foster carers

The majority of foster carers (83 per cent) had no direct experience of making a formal complaint. Most carers preferred to address problems through the various hierarchical levels within the department:

> *We've not used the complaints procedure. We've always gone through the levels with it . . . We've helped [young people] . . . put stuff in writing and sometimes put it to the area officer responsible.* (Foster carer)

Similarly, the majority of link workers we spoke to (56 per cent) had little experience of the complaints procedure being used. Most of the problems their carers encountered were generally resolved by other methods:

*We do a lot of problem solving before it gets to that point.* (Link worker)

*Ninety-nine per cent of the time . . . the problem solving that foster carers have is dealt with at an informal level . . . with the help of the support worker . . . Carers want to problem solve. They don't want to make an issue about things.* (Link worker)

Some link workers, however, spoke about the difficulties or their own apprehension about supporting a complaint against a colleague or senior manager:

*It didn't go to a formal complaint. It wasn't investigated . . . It's very hard for me to tell a colleague I don't think they're doing their job very well.* (Link worker)

*It's quite difficult to keep going back to an area manager telling them what they ought to have done. So we left it in the end.* (Link worker)

Nearly 40 per cent of foster carers felt the support they received from staff, and their own resourcefulness, meant problems did not become entrenched, thereby avoiding complaints. However, the majority spoke of the negative consequences of making a complaint, particularly the fear of repercussions. This ranged from anxiety that working relationships with social services staff would deteriorate, to fear of deregistration:

*My relationship with [the young person's] social worker isn't great and to complain about somebody you've got to work with . . . You have to be careful because you still have to work with them.* (Foster carer)

*A lot won't use [the complaints procedure] because they're too scared . . . They think if they complain then they'll end up not being able to foster.* (Foster carer)

Foster carers were also concerned that they might be viewed as a 'trouble maker' or have a 'bad mark' against them, or that complaining could have negative consequences for the young person:

*You get a lot of backlash if you actually say something and stand up for yourself . . . you get a bad name for yourself.* (Foster carer)

*It might be causing trouble for the child or maybe yourself.* (Foster carer)

Over 70 per cent of link workers also recognised the negative aspects of using the complaints procedure, reiterating the fears expressed by foster carers. There was a climate of disapproval within social services if foster carers tried to side-step accepted modes of problem solving. Making a complaint was generally seen to be an extreme measure on a par with disciplinary or child protection procedures. The complaints procedure was also seen to be an ineffective means of problem solving. It was regarded as too official, bureaucratic and cumbersome. Link workers in one authority reported carers' use of a 'Director's Hotline' (a dedicated answer service) as a much more immediate and efficient way of getting a response from senior management.

Foster carers who had experienced a complaints investigation were reported to have found the process intimidating. Link workers reported situations in which they themselves felt unlistened to by the department and felt foster carers were at an even greater disadvantage. One link worker described foster carers as being very small voices against a huge bureaucracy, and therefore unlikely to challenge social work practice or procedures.

Complaints from foster carers that managers were aware of tended to be about the way they had been treated by department, or about a specific children's social worker. Foster carers were generally looking for recognition of the difficulties they faced. But as one complaints officer highlighted:

> I don't think we're very good yet at feeding back lessons that come out of complaints. (Complaints officer)

One manager felt that the lack of evidence of any real positive change resulting from making a complaint discouraged foster carers from using the procedure. The isolated position of some foster carers was also seen as a contributing factor. The fact that some carers did not identify with the wider organisation meant they were unlikely to use mechanisms such as the complaints procedures even when they very unhappy with a situation.

One link worker for Asian foster carers also highlighted the difficulties connected with language. Given that foster carers' manuals were not translated into Asian languages in the authorities studied (despite having significant minority populations), foster carers who did not read English were unlikely to have knowledge of or access to the complaints procedure. The UK National Standards for Foster Care (National Foster Care Association, 1999) stress that provision should be made for people whose first language is not English, but we were not aware of detailed literature for foster carers being available in other languages.

Again the aspirations of The Children Act have not been realised. The complaints procedure clearly does not offer foster carers the effective avenue to air grievances as originally envisaged.

## Discussion

The complaints procedure has the potential to function not only as a problem solving tool, but also as a child protection safeguard and a source of management information. However, comments from those interviewed show little indication that the procedure has any impact on foster care.

### Problem solving

Neither young people nor foster carers saw the complaints procedure as an accessible or even useful tool in problem solving. The majority of young people, and about one-third of foster carers, had little or no knowledge of the procedure at all. Those who did either chose alternative ways of resolving problems or highlighted fears about potential consequences of using the procedure.

Most young people and foster carers were confident that any problems they had could be resolved with the help of social workers and link workers without recourse to a formal complaints procedure. As we saw in Chapter 4, this is a very effective process for the majority of young people in foster care. For the minority unsupported group, however, where the core network of support is weak, reliance on carers and social workers does not offer these young people an effective means of solving problems. If communication with foster carers or social workers is poor, the complaints procedure could potentially offer young people a valuable alternative outside the limited core triangle. However, comments from all those interviewed show this to be unlikely in practice.

A climate of disapproval within social services was described. Social workers appeared reluctant to share information with young people, and foster carers felt they had to stick to accepted hierarchical routes of problems solving. Carers expressed disquiet at the idea of complaining about people they had to work with, or even feared deregistration if they made a complaint. For a foster carer to make a complaint (or support a young person to make a complaint), they would have to feel substantial dissatisfaction or anger for them to face such institutional disapproval. For a young person to seek support from their carers to make a complaint, they would not only have to overcome their own lack of knowledge and apprehension, but would also have to overcome their foster carer's resistance. It is little surprise then that the complaints procedure is so seldom used in foster care.

## Child protection safeguards

When introduced by The Children Act 1989, the Representations and Complaints Procedure was intended to act as one of the safeguards for looked after young people. In his report of the safeguards for children living away from home, Sir William Utting quotes a survey in which 305 cases of abuse in foster placements were found to be substantiated (Utting, 1997 p.35). In his review he says that fostering is essentially a private activity and it is hard to assess how effectively safeguards for the protection of children are working. This study demonstrates that the substantial lack of knowledge and reluctance of young people in foster placements to use the complaints procedure means the procedure is not working as a child protection safeguard for young people in foster care, despite repeated evidence for its need (*see* Waterhouse, 2000).

Young people in this study identified abuse or mistreatment as a potential reason to use the complaints procedure. They were clearly aware of issues about their own safety and protection, and need to know that they have both the right and the means to complain.

We have seen that a minority of young people in foster care (up to 15 per cent), are likely to feel unsupported in their placements. This includes those with persistent poor relationships and those where interruption in support is temporary. Without links outside the core triangle of support, abuse or mistreatment can persist undetected and unchallenged, as graphically illustrated by young people's stories in *Shout to be Heard* (Growney, 1998) a report from Voice of the Child in Care. The fears that keep young people from disclosing abuse or mistreatment in their own families apply equally to those in substitute families. National inquiries and reviews have consistently highlighted the need for child-friendly, accessible complaints procedures to enhance the provision of safeguards that young people are entitled to (*see* Kahan and Levy, 1991; Utting, 1997; Waterhouse, 2000).

### Management information

The young people we spoke to mentioned the provision, or lack of provision, of services by social workers as another possible situation where they might make a formal complaint. The evidence from the young people and foster carers in this study suggests that, in practice, young people are more likely to be dissatisfied about services or lack of services from their social workers than about the standards of care offered by foster carers. Social services staff, however, were quick to assume complaints in foster care meant complaints against foster carers. They appeared less open to the idea that young people could be empowered to challenge provision of services by social workers.

As we saw in the previous chapter, problems that young people or foster carers experience may be discussed at line management level or at reviews, but comments about dissatisfaction with social work services are not collated or fed back to managers in any coherent form. The rare formal complaint from a young person in foster care, or from their carer, cannot therefore be put into any context. More systematic logging of dissatisfaction, whether or not termed a complaint, would provide management with a much fuller picture and inform changes and developments in fostering.

## Conclusion

The complaints procedure in foster care simply isn't working very well. Local authorities are obliged by law to publicise their procedures. Clearly, this publicity is not reaching all young people in foster care effectively. Empowering young people to make use of the complaints procedure offers them an alternative if their problems are not being resolved in other ways. It also strengthens child protection safeguards, giving young people permission to speak out when they feel mistreated.

But this empowerment is hindered by an entrenched climate of disapproval within social services about the use of the complaints procedure by both young people and foster carers. Introducing child-friendly literature, good publicity or children's rights posts will have little effect if this negative culture within social services remains unchallenged.

# Summary

### Young people

- Over half of young people in foster care (55 per cent) have no knowledge of the complaints procedure.

- Although 45 per cent of young people in foster care have some knowledge that they can complain, they are not necessarily aware of a formal procedure.

- Knowledge about the complaints procedure varies between local authorities. But there is no difference in knowledge between age groups. Teenagers are no better informed than 8–12-year-olds, despite the perceptions of social workers.

- Social workers identify their own gatekeeping of information as contributing to young people's lack of knowledge.

- Social workers are far less likely to support and encourage young people in foster care to use the complaints procedure, compared with those in residential care.

- As well as young people's lack of knowledge, young people, foster carers and social services staff highlight the differences in culture, environment and quality of care between residential care and foster care as the main reasons why young people in foster care rarely use the complaints procedure. They believe that care is good so there is less to complain about.

- However, young people, foster carers and social workers also highlight young people's fears of the consequences of complaining, particularly the very real fears that young people have about being moved to residential care if they 'cause trouble'.

- Social services staff tend to look unfavourably on the use of the complaints procedure in foster care, seeing the procedure as adversarial and unhelpful in problem solving and possibly contributing to placement breakdown.

- Social services staff are more likely to assume complaints in foster care mean complaints about foster carers. They appear less open to the idea that young people could challenge the provision of services by social workers.

- Overall there is very poor collation of informal complaints from young people in foster care and no collation of complaints raised at reviews. Management therefore has very little information about the level and type of complaints raised by young people in foster care.

### Foster carers

- Some 68 per cent of foster carers are aware of the complaints procedure, but this awareness encompasses a wide variation in actual knowledge. There is little variation in knowledge between local authorities.

- This leaves nearly one-third of foster carers claiming to have little or no knowledge about the complaints procedure.

- Link workers also acknowledge a wide variation in foster carers' knowledge.

- More than 80 per cent of foster carers have no experience of making a complaint or encouraging a young person to make a complaint.

- A minority of foster carers (less than 20 per cent) have made a complaint of some kind, but not necessarily via the complaints procedure.

- Issues complained about by foster carers in all local authorities focused almost entirely on the services provided to young people by social workers. This is supported by the responses of link workers.

- Foster carers and link workers highlight the positive aspects of problem solving as one of the main reasons foster carers rarely use the complaints procedure. They rely on the commitment and ability of foster carers and social services staff to sort out problems as they arise.

- However, the majority of foster carers and link workers acknowledge that fear of possible consequences contributes significantly to foster carers' reluctance to use the procedure.

- There is a climate of disapproval within social services if foster carers try to side-step accepted modes of problem solving.

- A formal complaint made by a foster carer is regarded by both foster carers and social services staff as an extreme measure, on a par with disciplinary and child protection procedures.

# 8

# POLICY AND PRACTICE ISSUES

## Overview

Overall, the findings of this study are positive. The majority of the young people we consulted with feel well supported in their placements. For the most part they are looked after by very committed and resourceful foster carers, for whom young people have a high regard. In addition, most young people feel well enough supported by their social workers.

## Well supported and unsupported groups

Our major finding is the division of young people into two groups, which we have termed 'well-supported' and 'unsupported'. Although the majority of young people feel well supported, this leaves a worrying minority who feel they are not. The unsupported young people are likely to be a fluctuating group and are not easily identified. In terms of problem solving they are vulnerable and do not have a consistent adult to turn to. Social workers recognise that young people are not always placed with carers who can meet their needs and therefore the role of social workers becomes particularly important in these cases. Foster carers also recognise that young people are not always well supported by social workers, and this can exacerbate attempts to problem solve.

## Young people's problem solving network

### Support network

We have identified that problem solving for young people takes place within a core triangle of support comprising the young person, their foster carers and the social worker. This is a successful model for the well supported majority, but does not meet the needs of the unsupported group. This network needs to be expanded for young people so that they have a much broader choice of where to seek support.

### Birth family

Clearly birth families can play an important role and, as we have seen, the welfare of their families and levels of contact are major issues of concern for young people. Social workers need to be aware of who within the birth family can continue to offer the young person consistent support. Social workers need to be actively promoting such relationships in the spirit of *Working Together to Safeguard Children* (Department of Health, 2000).

## Peers

Peer friendships should not be undervalued. The looked after system focuses heavily on adults being seen as the ones who support young people. But the young people we consulted have said how, at times, the only people they seek support from are their friends. Nationally there is a lack of 'joined-up' thinking between social services and education departments about meeting the needs of looked after young people. Where attention is focused on schools it is often around academic achievement or challenging behaviour. Yet school is where young people develop friendships and social skills, and learn to be valued (or rejected). In this, social work seems to lack a 'holistic' view of young people's worlds. Peers can provide young people with safe relationships in which to explore ways of dealing with their problems, especially if they distrust adults or feel adults have a different agenda. Social workers should work with young people to identify who their supportive friends are and should encourage and facilitate these relationships. Where young people have moved to a new area or changed schools, valuable friendships are sometimes lost, as the young people in this study have confirmed.

## Schools

All schools have a designated teacher responsible for ensuring that the needs of looked after children are met within the school environment. These and others with pastoral responsibilities can offer young people in foster care an alternative source of support. The establishment of organised peer support networks, peer advocacy and mentoring schemes within schools may also benefit young people who do not feel able to confide in either their foster carer or social worker.

## Independent services

Independent support from children's rights services, advocacy services or independent visitor schemes were rarely mentioned by young people, foster carers or social services staff. Children's rights services exist in only two of the three local authorities studied, and in neither of these were the organisations active with young people in foster care. There is considerable potential for broadening the work of children's rights and advocacy services to engage with young people in foster care, offering yet another choice of contact and support for young people.

## Natural allies

Other adults such as teachers, neighbours, taxi drivers, dinner ladies, etc. may all provide alternative support for young people outside the recognised core triangle. What is needed is for social workers to identify who young people's natural allies are and actively support these relationships, thereby broadening the options available to young people.

### Managers

We have seen that foster carers and social services staff recognise an extended problem solving network involving successive layers of management, but this is only accessible to young people through their foster carers or social workers. Social services managers need to open up direct lines of communication with young people. There needs to be a culture that sees this communication as friendly, widely acceptable and not limited to the 'bad' things.

## Change and stability

Consistent with other studies, we found that many of the young people in our study had experienced recent changes in placement. The damaging effects of frequent moves are well known and the Government has set targets to reduce the number of placements young people experience. In addition, many of the young people had experienced recent changes of social worker. When familiar modes of support are missing or interrupted, even young people within the usually well supported group can find themselves struggling to find the level of support they need. Much more attention should be paid to the continuity of the social worker. Social services departments should take this into account in terms of recruitment of social workers, retention policies and the impact reorganisation has on young people. Identification of natural allies as suggested above would help provide young people with longer-term advocates who may be able to offer greater continuity than the professionals can.

## Role of foster carers

Our study shows that the majority of foster carers have a central role to play in problem solving for young people. They demonstrate considerable competence, patience and resourcefulness in working with young people and professionals. Many of their skills are gained through experience. Our study attracted a disproportionate number of very experienced foster carers (75 per cent fostering for more than five years). In Scotland, 52 per cent of carers had fostered for less than five years (Triseliotis et al., 2000). Young people and social workers acknowledged that not all carers were as skilled and supportive. Foster carers need to be adequately trained from the outset to equip even newly registered foster carers with the skills needed in problem solving. They should be openly acknowledged and valued by social services for their problem solving skills and all foster carers should receive ongoing support, training and constant provision of up-to-date information to help them in their role. Our foster carers recognised their limitations and indicated their willingness to develop problem solving skills.

Foster carers should be empowered in their role of advocating for young people, particularly where young people's views differ from their social workers'. There needs to be clarification of roles and expectations so that carers do not feel trapped between doing their best for the young person they care for and trying not to 'upset' social services. This could possibly be done through a contract system that recognises carers as partners in the provision of services. Such issues feed into the national debate about the 'professional' status of foster carers.

Foster carers also need training in how to recognise 'detachment' early on. A high proportion of young people in our study attempt to resolve domestic problems themselves. While this may reflect young people's skills, it may also mask the unsupported group. Domestic problems may be the first indicators that all is not well. Foster carers also tend to address domestic problems 'in-house'. Although most do so with competence, there are cultural pressures for them to present themselves as capable and coping, and asking for help may be seen as 'failure'. Foster carers should be encouraged, enabled and trained to recognise when their supportive relationships with young people are not working well. This needs to be openly shared without the fear of appearing inadequate. In this way carers and social workers can work together to find the young person the support they need and to seek to broaden their supportive contacts, as suggested earlier.

## Direct work with young people

Our study reinforces the importance of direct work skills with young people. Social workers and foster carers need to develop their skills in terms of listening to young people and responding to their needs and concerns. With nearly 40 per cent of social workers finding it difficult to engage with some young people, this should act as a trigger to actively look for alternatives rather than 'closing down' or just accepting that the young person does not want to talk to them. Carers in this study have noted that some direct work between young people and their social workers comprises little more than social workers supervising contact with their families. With visits to young people spaced at one to two months apart, social workers need very good direct work skills to ensure visits are constructive and effective for young people.

## The social worker's role

A number of our findings point to the centrality of the social worker's role. Social workers play a key part in the core triangle of support for young people and in support for foster carers. They also act as a feedback route to managers for both young people and carers. Our evidence identifies the quality of social work intervention as being the single most influential factor in determining the outcomes of problem solving for young people and carers. Social workers need to acknowledge the key role they play within fostering and they require support – through supervision and training – to fulfil this role effectively.

The importance of contact with their parents, siblings and wider networks emerges as a consistent issue for young people in foster care. It is an issue where young people and carers expect social workers to be proactive. This again needs to be highlighted in training and supervision. Contact issues also need to be raised frequently in planning meetings and reviews. Young people do change allegiances and, where problem solving is concerned, the confidant of six months ago may not be the confidant of today.

Even though two-thirds of looked after young people are placed with foster carers, young people in foster care often account for only a small minority of individual social workers' caseloads. Workers can lack knowledge and expertise of fostering issues. Social worker appraisals need to identify where skills are lacking and ensure workers develop the expertise needed in this field. There is also a need to emphasise this role in professional social work training, perhaps involving young people and foster carers in training programmes. Linked to this issue is the fact that about 20 per cent of foster carers feel unhappy with the role undertaken by social workers. Foster carers should feel comfortable in raising such issues with link workers and managers, and in reviews. *UK National Standards for Foster Care* (National Foster Care Association, 1999) and *Working Together to Safeguard Children* (Department of Health, 2000) stress the need for this partnership and managers need to know when it is failing.

Social workers acknowledge that young people are sometimes placed in unsatisfactory placements due to lack of choice and the scarcity of foster carers in general. Taking this as an indicator that the young person is likely to fall within the unsupported group, social workers need to be proactive to ensure compensatory support systems are in place. On one hand this acknowledges a failure in the system to find suitable placements, but it also acknowledges the need to create a 'survival' strategy for the duration of the placement – which could be a long time if alternatives are in short supply. This requires being up front about the corporate parenting responsibilities of the authority rather than maintaining that any placement is better than none.

## Feedback and influence of young people's views

Foster carers, social workers and statutory childcare reviews are identified as the routes via which young people's views can be fed back to social services managers. However, doubts were expressed in our study about how effective these routes are.

Foster carers need to be encouraged and enabled to act as true advocates for young people. Carers need to be able to distinguish between when they are putting forward what young people wish them to say and when they are offering their own views and opinions. This may sometimes be hard to distinguish and requires not only specific training but also a commitment on the part of social services to respect carers' role in advocacy.

Social workers need to listen closely to young people and need to take responsibility for passing on their views. The type of information passed on must be broadened significantly to encompass the whole child and not just be a focus on difficulties.

Reviewing systems need to be much more child-focused, to encourage and enable young people to take part. They need to move away from their adult-focused model to one that truly meets the needs of young people. If young people do not feel able to voice their views in a meeting full of adults, then alternatives should be found. Young people may benefit from having an advocate who may be their foster carer, friend, children's rights worker or other natural ally. Meetings can be restricted to those individuals chosen by the young person, with other people's views being sought separately if necessary. Imagination, creativity and flexibility must be used, and in making changes social services should listen closely to what young people want. Reviews do not have to be prescriptive. They can be tailored to the needs of individuals. But the will, determination and resources to make the process work effectively for young people have to come from the local authorities. As corporate parents they have the responsibility to ensure young people are heard.

Many of the findings in this study suggest the lack of a systematic method for feeding back the views of young people to managers. This is particularly important in terms of the aims of Quality Protects. The views of young people need to be systematically collected through a variety of methods, which might include surveys, consultation groups, collection of complaints, collation of information from reviews and supervision, etc. These views should then be fed into management processes to ensure fostering services are responsive to young people's expressed views.

Local authority councillors have a clear role under Quality Protects to act as corporate parents to children and young people in the looked after system. They need to develop ways of familiarising themselves with the needs of young people in foster care. They should be asking officers to provide them with information about young people's views and experience, and should find ways of hearing the voices of young people in foster care directly. Information should be provided to young people about councillors, their responsibilities and how they can contact them.

## Team working

In common with those in most local authorities nationally, the fostering teams within each of the local authorities in our study are divided into two distinct lines of management: the fostering unit responsible for family placement and support, and field social work. These distinct lines only merge at senior management level (*see* Diagram 1, page 8).

It has been shown that problem solving and the participation and influence of young people and foster carers is most effective where there is good team working between all concerned: where young people, carers, social workers and link workers communicate well, rely on and support each other, and where there is mutual respect for each other's skills. But rather than being built into the organisational structure, such team working relies on the skills and commitment of individuals. Local authorities need to ensure appropriate links are made between fostering units and field social work teams, and that there are forums through which information is freely exchanged, collated and passed on to senior managers and policy makers.

## The complaints procedure

This study confirms earlier findings in terms of the complaint system being fairly marginal as a problem solving mechanism for looked after young people, and particularly so for those in foster care. With the majority of young people in this study having little or no awareness of the complaints procedure, there are clearly improvements to be made in publicity and the targeting of information to young people in foster care. UK National Standards for Foster Care are not being met in regard to this issue (*see* National Foster Care Association, 1999, para. 25.3). Knowledge does vary between local authorities and much can be learnt from the successful strategies employed by others. Knowledge among foster carers was also variable and written material available only in English in the local authorities studied. Here again, paragraphs 25.4 and 25.5 of the UK National Standards for Foster Care fail to be met. Each of the local authorities studied has substantial ethnic minority populations. As a matter of priority, essential information for foster carers should be available in relevant minority languages.

The network available to young people for problem solving needs to be broadened beyond the foster carer and social worker, particularly for those likely to fall within the unsupported group. The complaints procedure offers one alternative to young people, but evidence indicates that for most this option is inaccessible. Steps need to be taken to improve access and acceptability for young people to use the complaints procedure, such as those suggested in *Cause for Complaint* (Wallis and Frost, 1998).

Children's rights services and advocacy services can play important roles in providing advice, information and support to young people. Utting (1998) commented that young people were unlikely to make effective use of the complaints procedure unless they had good advocacy to support them through the process. Two of the local authorities studied have children's rights services and the third employs a specific complaints officer for children. These services, however, are targeted almost exclusively at young people in residential care. Models of working with young people in residential homes are not necessarily transferable to working within foster care. Local authorities need to look seriously and creatively at how to address the gap in services on offer to those in foster care.

The culture of institutional disapproval within social services over the use of the complaints procedure, particularly by foster carers, needs to be challenged at all levels in the organisation. Young people and foster carers identified their fear of possible consequences as contributing to their reluctance to use the procedure. Social workers, link workers and line managers especially need to provide information to young people and carers, and create an atmosphere of permission and acceptance within their working practices. For young people wishing to enlist the support of their carers in making a complaint, they not only have to overcome their own apprehensions but also their foster carer's reluctance. Such obstacles offer an explanation as to why the complaints procedure is so rarely used by young people in foster care.

The complaints procedure is intended as a child protection safeguard, yet there seems to be a reluctance to 'politicise' young people in terms of access to rights and information. Professionals should not take the existence of a complaints procedure as an acceptance that a safeguard is in place. Local authorities cannot be satisfied that they can safeguard young people if they do not equip young people with the information to safeguard themselves.

## Multiple perspectives

Our study shows that although there is often consensus of view, sometimes young people, foster carers, social workers and link workers have different perspectives on the same issue. Material from this study lends itself to use as part of joint training where these issues and differing perspectives may be shared and discussed.

## Recommendations

- Social services should be proactive in expanding the support network for young people in foster care. This may include dependable family members, young people's friends, peer support schemes, supportive teachers and independent services (such as children's rights services, advocacy services and independent visitors). Social services should identify who young people's natural allies are and support these relationships. Social services managers need to open up direct lines of communication with young people in foster care.
- Social services departments need to pay greater attention to the continuity of social workers for young people. This should be taken into account in terms of recruitment and retention policies and plans for reorganisation of services.
- Social services need to openly acknowledge and value the central role that foster carers play in problem solving. All carers from the outset should be equipped – through training and support – with the skills needed.
- Foster carers should be trained and empowered to act as advocates for young people. There needs to be clarification of roles and expectations – possibly achieved through a contact system that recognises carers as partners in the provision of services.
- Social services should promote the importance of direct work skills with young people, ensuring social workers and foster carers continue to develop their skills in listening and responding to young people's needs and concerns.
- Social workers need to acknowledge the key role they play within fostering, in terms of problem solving, maintaining family contact and identifying natural allies.
- The key role of social workers in fostering needs to be emphasised in professional training.
- Young people should be informed of the roles and responsibilities of both foster carers and social services, so that they are clear who to approach in different circumstances if they have a problem.

- With young people in foster care accounting for only a small minority of social workers' caseloads, social services must ensure social workers develop their expertise in this field.

- Social workers should take greater responsibility in passing on the views of young people to managers.

- Review systems need to be much more child focused to encourage and enable young people to take part, and voice their views and concerns.

- Local authorities should ensure appropriate links are made between fostering units and field social work teams, and that there are forums through which information is freely exchanged and passed on to senior managers and policy makers.

- Social services departments must establish systematic methods for collecting and collating the views of young people in foster care from all sources. These views need to be fed into management processes to ensure fostering services are responsive to young people's expressed views.

- Information about the complaints procedure should be specifically targeted at young people in foster care and their foster carers to ensure they have knowledge and access to the complaints procedure.

- The culture of institutional disapproval regarding the use of the complaints procedure needs to be challenged at all levels in the local authority. Most importantly, disapproval at social worker, link worker and line management level needs to be actively challenged as a priority.

- Local authority councillors need to take on board their responsibilities as corporate parents with regard to young people in foster care, ensuring they make themselves aware of the views of young people in foster care.

# BIBLIOGRAPHY

Aldgate, J. and Hawley, D. (1986) 'Helping foster families through disruption'. *Adoption and Fostering*, vol. 10, no. 2: pp. 44–49.

Aldgate, J. and Hawley, D. (1986) 'Preventing disruption in long-term foster care'. *Adoption and Fostering*, vol.10, no. 3, pp. 23–30.

Baldry, S. and Kemmis, J. (1998) 'What it is like to be looked after by a local authority'. *British Journal of Social Work*, vol. 28, no. 1, pp. 129–36.

Berridge, D. (1997) *Foster Care: A Research Review*. London: The Stationery Office.

Berridge, D. and Cleaver, H. (1987) *Foster Home Breakdown*. Oxford: Blackwell.

Bond, H. (1999) 'Hear their Voice'. *Community Care*, 9–15 September 1999.

Bond, H. and Pickerden, J. (eds) (2000) *The Need to Know. Meeting the information and communication needs of children in public care. Research findings and recommendations for good practice*. London: Who Cares? Trust.

Colton, M. (1989) 'Foster and residential children's perceptions of the environment'. *British Journal of Social Work*, vol. 19, no. 3, pp. 217–33.

Connolly, J. (1996) 'Scaling the wall'. *Community Care*, no. 1128, pp. 26–27.

Dalrymple, J. and Payne, M. (1994) *They Listened to Him: A Report on the Evaluation Project of the Advice, Advocacy and Representations Services for Children (ASC)*. ASC/ Manchester Metropolitan University.

Department of Health (1991) *Statutory Instrument 894 – Representations Procedure (Children) Regulations*. London: HMSO.

Department of Health (1998) *Modernising Social Services*. London: The Stationery Office.

Department of Health (1999) *The Children Act Report, 1995–1999*. London: The Stationery Office.

Department of Health (2000) *Working Together to Safeguard Children*. The Stationery Office.

Department of Health (2000) 'Listen and learn'. *Community Care*, November 2000 (Supplement on Quality Protects Initiative).

The Dolphin Project (1993) *Answering Back: Report by young people being looked after on The Children Act 1989*. Buchanan, A. *et al*. Southampton: Southampton University, Dept. of Social Work Studies.

Fletcher, B. (1993) *Not Just a Name: the views of young people in foster and residential care*. London: NCC and Who Cares? Trust.

Frost, N., Mills, S. and Stein, M. (1999) *Understanding Residential Child Care*. Aldershot: Arena.

Fry, E. (1999) The Way Forward in *The RHP Companion to Foster Care*. Lyme Regis: Russell House Publishing.

Grimshaw, R. and Sinclair, R. (1997) The participation of young people and their parents at review meetings. Chapter 6 in *Planning to Care: Regulation, Procedure and Practice under The Children Act 1989*. London: National Children's Bureau.

Growney, T. (ed.) (1998) *Sometimes You've Got to Shout To Be Heard: stories from young people in care about getting heard, using advocates and making complaints*. London: Voice for the Child in Care.

Heywood, J. (1978) *Children in Care: the development of the service for the deprived child*. London: Routledge Kegan Paul.

Hogan, G. and Sinclair, R. (1997) 'Children and young people's participation in reviews'. In G. Horgan and R. Sinclair (eds) *Planning for Children in Care in Northern Ireland*. London: National Children's Bureau.

Ibidun, B. (2000) 'Give children a chance'. *Community Care*, 13–19 April 2000.

Johnson, P. R., Yoken, C. and Voss, R. (1994) 'Family foster care placement. The child's perspective'. *Child Welfare*, LXXIV, 5, pp. 959–74.

Kahan, B. and Levy, A. (1991) *The Pindown Experience and the Protection of Children. Report of the Staffordshire child care inquiry*. Staffordshire County Council.

Kelly, G. and Gilligan, R. (eds) (2000) *Issues in Foster Care – Policy, Practice and Research*. London: Jessica Kingsley.

Kufeldt, K. (1984) 'Listening to children – who cares?' *British Journal of Social Work*, no. 14.

Lynes, D. and Goddard, J. (1995) *View from the Front: The Users' View of Child Care in Norfolk*. Norfolk County Council Social Services Department.

MacLeod, M. (1996) *Children Living away from Home*. London: Childline.

McAuley, C. (1996) *Children in Long Term Foster Care: Emotional and Social Development*. Aldershot: Avebury.

McTeigue, D. (1998) 'The use of focus groups in exploring children's experiences of life in care'. In Hogan, D. and Gilligan, R. (eds) *Researching Children's Experience: Qualitative Approaches (Proceedings of Conference 27.5.97)*. Dublin: The Children's Research Centre, Trinity College Dublin.

Morris, S. and Wheatley, H. (1994) *Time to Listen: The experiences of Young People in Foster and Residential Care*. London: Childline.

National Foster Care Association (1999) *UK National Standards for Foster Care*, London: NFCA.

Pithouse, A., Young, C. and Butler, I. (1994) *All Wales Review: Local Authority Fostering Services*. Cardiff: University of Wales College of Cardiff, School of Social and Administrative Studies.

Rowe, J., Cain, H., Hundleby, M. and Keane, A. (1984) *Long-term Foster Care*. London: Batsford.

Ruegger, M. and Rayfield, L. (1999) 'The nature and dilemmas of fostering in the nineties'. In *The RHP Companion to Foster Care*. Lyme Regis: Russell House Publishing.

Schofield, G. (2000) 'Parental responsibility and parenting – the needs of accommodated children in long-term foster care'. *Child and Family Law*, vol.12, no. 4, pp. 345–61.

Schofield, G. and Thoburn, J. (1996) *Child Protection: The Voice of the Child in Decision Making*. London: Institute of Public Policy Research.

Shaw, C. (1998) *Remember my Messages*. London: The Who Cares? Trust.

Sinclair, I. and Gibbs, I. (1996) *The Quality of Care in Children's Homes*. London: Department of Health.

Social Services Inspectorate (1996) *Inspection of Local Authority Fostering 1995–1996: National Summary Report*. London: Department of Health.

Social Services Inspectorate (1998) *Someone Else's Children. Inspection of Planning and Decision Making for Children Looked After and The Safety of Children Looked After*. Wetherby: Department of Health.

Thomas, N. and O'Kane, C. (1998) *Children and Decision Making: a summary report*. University of Wales Swansea: International Centre for Childhood Studies.

Thomas, N. and O'Kane, C. (1998) 'When children's wishes and feelings clash with their best interests'. *The International Journal of Children's Rights*, vol. 6 1998, pp. 137–154.

Thomas, N. and O'Kane, C. (1988) 'The reality of participation in decisions for children who are "looked after".' Paper presented to 'Exchanging Visions' Conference, University of Bradford 22–24 April 1998.

Templeton, J. (1998) 'Listening to looked after children: the government's response to the Utting Report'. *Child Right*, December 1998, no. 152, pp. 10–11.

Triseliotis, J., Borland, M. and Hill, M. (2000) *Delivering Foster Care*. London: British Agencies for Adoption and Fostering.

Utting, W. (1991) *Children in the Public Care – A Review of Residential Child Care*. London: HMSO.

Utting, W. (1997) *People Like Us: The Report of Safeguards for Children Living Away From Home*. London: HMSO.

Wallis, L. and Frost, N. (1998) *Cause for Complaint: The Complaints Procedure for Young People in Care*. London: The Children's Society.

Waterhouse, S. (1997) *The Organisation of Fostering Services in England*. London: NFCA.

Waterhouse (2000) *Lost in Care. The Report of the Tribunal of Inquiry into Abuse of Children in Care in the former County Council areas of Gwynedd and Clwyd since 1974.* London: The Stationery Office.

Wheal, A. (ed.) (1999) *The RHP Companion to Foster Care.* Lyme Regis: Russell House Publishing.